The Great Silver Bull

Crush Inflation and Profit as the Dollar Dies

Peter Krauth

Publisher's Note

To my wife, for her infinite patience and understanding,

my parents, for their endless support,

and my father for introducing me to silver,

and investing outside the mainstream.

Thanks to

Sarah Jamieson, whose expert guidance and skillful help during the entire process have been invaluable,

Gwen Preston, for her wonderful and constant support,

Bill Patalon III, who suggested and encouraged me to write this book,

and the many others who provided feedback, insight, or otherwise contributed towards this effort.

The Great Silver Bull

**Crush Inflation and
Profit as the Dollar Dies**

Peter Krauth

Table of Contents

Foreword

Silver is the most versatile and indispensable of all metals. It's essential in our industrial economy and it's been used as money for millennia. Today, silver is more widely used than ever, especially in the green economy where silver's electrical conductivity makes it essential for solar power and virtually all digital products. But silver's future price action is really tied to its greatest use as a store of value - as investment.

The global explosion of money printing and debt in recent years has created predictable increases in inflation and debasement of fiat currencies. This is a perfect environment for precious metals to do what they've done for thousands of years -protect wealth and preserve value. Silver and gold have increased in price, often spectacularly, throughout history whenever conditions are like they are today.

The Great Silver Bull explains in detail why silver is a great way to hedge against devaluing paper money, why it should outperform gold in today's financial environment and why every investor should own physical silver and silver mining and exploration companies. It's a comprehensive review of the case for investing in silver to protect everyone's wealth and purchasing power.

In 1994, I founded Pan American Silver Corp. to take advantage of the same silver fundamentals that Peter Krauth writes about in this book. Silver then was out of fashion as an investment class, the silver price was low, silver mine investments were minimal, and investors were focusing on other products. Our focus was to build one of the world's great silver mining companies and we succeeded - Pan American Silver is today the world's second largest primary silver mining company.

Peter explains why silver mining stocks have such explosive

investment returns in bull markets. Pan American certainly is an example of this - its price rose from a low of $2.52 in 2001 when the silver price bottomed at just over $4 an ounce, to a high of $42.53 in 2008, a capital gain of 1,587%. These are the kind of investment gains that are possible when silver really takes off.

Silver and gold investments currently make up just 0.5% of the total U.S. savings and investment market. The average of the last three decades is 1.5%. This might be explained by the extraordinary returns that have been made in conventional investment markets over the past decade or so. But as inflation rises, as central banks try to tighten, as conventional investment classes decline in value, and as investors increasingly realize they need to look at asset classes like gold and silver that have held their value throughout history, I expect overall allocations to return to their long-term average. This could triple the demand for precious metals across the board - for physical metal, ETFs, and mining and exploration stocks.

Silver is not only a great investment class - it's also beautiful. Silver is the most reflective metal, so it both radiates beauty and reflects beauty. Whether you own silver metal or silver stocks, I hope you savor this beauty and get some kind of "extra" enjoyment from owning, directly or indirectly, such an amazing metal.

I'm convinced we are in a long-term bull market for silver and gold, and I expect investment returns in precious metals will outperform all other investment classes for the foreseeable future. Peter's book is an excellent introduction to why this is likely - I hope you enjoy it and take its lessons to heart.

ROSS J. BEATY
CHAIRMAN EMERITUS
PAN AMERICAN SILVER CORP.

Introduction: Silver is Your Generational Opportunity

"I spent my entire academic career studying the Great Depression. The depression may have started because of a stock market crash, but what hit the general economy was a disruption of credit. Average citizens unable to borrow money, to do anything. To buy a home, start a business, stock their shelves. Credit has the ability to build a modern economy, but lack of credit has the ability to destroy it, swiftly and absolutely. If we do not act, boldly and immediately, we will replay the depression of the 1930s, only this time it will be far, far worse. We don't do this now, we won't have an economy on Monday."

FED CHAIRMAN BEN BERNANKE (PLAYED BY PAUL GIAMATTI)
HBO DOCUDRAMA *TOO BIG TO FAIL* (2011)

Ask anyone and they'll tell you that the COVID-19 pandemic changed everything - forever.

And they'd be right.

Or ... almost right.

The "Great Pandemic" changed the world technologically (with remote-work applications and in biotech with telehealth and with new vaccine know-how). It changed the world geopolitically (forever altering the rapport between Washington and Beijing). It shifted things socially (with millions of people reexamining "what really mattered" to them - a bit of social soul-searching that led to the "Great Resignation").

But I'd argue - strongly - that it didn't have the same "change-agent" impact financially.

That change started more than a decade ago - following the Financial Crisis of 2008-09, and the Great Recession that followed.

During *that* crisis, nearly $20 trillion in household wealth was eviscerated - including $7.4 trillion in stock-market wealth (an average of nearly $70,000 per household). Not only did the stock market (as measured by the Standard & Poor's 500) freefall nearly 40% in 2008 alone, but U.S. housing prices also dropped by an average of 40% - with even bigger declines in some metro regions.

The setup and catalysts for that worldwide wealth disaster are complex, subject to debate and warrant a deeper discussion than we need to have here. But one thing is clear and not open to debate: It was a catastrophe of epic proportions - one that brought the global financial system to the brink of collapse.

And it marked the twisting open of the Great Liquidity Spigot.

As that line from the HBO docudrama, I cited at the start of this introduction illustrates, U.S. Federal Reserve Chairman Ben Bernanke, U.S. Treasury Secretary Hank Paulson and others in power at the time understood that - to get the financial system off the ledge - they needed to avoid the credit miscues of the Great Depression, and pump liquidity into the economy.

Indeed, Bernanke said that "importantly, in the 1930s, in the Great Depression, the Federal Reserve, despite its mandate, was quite passive and, as a result, [the] financial crisis became very severe [and] lasted essentially from 1929 to 1933."

Starting in December 2008, in operations that spanned a good six years, the U.S. central bank boosted its bond holdings by $3.7 trillion, meaning its balance sheet zoomed past $4.5 trillion.

Few of us realized it then, but that marked a crucial turning point in history - one that will shape our future for decades.

This was the start of what's known as "Modern Monetary Theory," and it's seductive in its allure for one very simple reason: It's an easy "fix" for the problems of today - with little concern about the fallout tomorrow.

But that's the playbook in use now. And that's the playbook global financial leaders resorted to when the "next" crisis took hold.

The COVID-19 Pandemic crisis.

In early 2020.

Governments mandated most businesses to close. Other than hospitals, grocery stores, pharmacies, and a few other essential services, nearly all economic activity ground to a complete halt.

It felt surreal. Then things got even weirder.

Over the following days and weeks, I watched in real-time on my computer screen as stock markets suffered their fastest crash ever. The S&P 500 index dropped from a record high, losing 30% in just 22 trading days - the fastest bear market in history.

The human toll was dreadful - and the personal stories heartbreaking.

The healthcare system was overwhelmed. Global travel was halted. The worldwide supply chain seized up like a motor with no oil.

And the money-printing began anew - to a degree never seen

before.

The following infographic from *Forbes* (using data from several sources) illustrates U.S. financial fiscal surplus or deficit from June 30, 1901, to Sept. 30, 2020.

U.S. Federal Budget (Surplus or Deficit)
June 1901 - Sept. 2020

Source: Forbes

As you can see, throughout most of the 1900s - right up into the first part of the 1970s - receipts and spending at the federal level were pretty much in line. Even through the two world wars and the Great Depression.

But then came the abandonment of the "gold standard" and Washington was off to the races from a spending standpoint.

But the real loss of control came with Modern Monetary Theory - which has seen U.S. debt skyrocket like never before. By the middle of 2021, U.S. debt had climbed past the $28 trillion mark - having soared $5 trillion in a mere 14 months, **according to** *Forbes*.

Even before some of the financial packages that followed, the national debt will approach $89 trillion by 2029 according to

USDebtClock.org. That would put America's debt-to-GDP ratio at 277%. That's more than the 272% that the moribund Japan faces right now.

And this isn't just an American problem - it's a global issue. Worldwide debt has soared to $296 trillion - a $36 trillion surge in less than two years.

All that money being thrown at Wall Street and Main Street has *seemed* to help. Unemployment soared with people essentially forced to stay home, while stocks recovered within just six months. Things looked better but, behind the scenes, they were not.

In the last two decades, the world's money supply has exploded by five times.

And it's far from done.

Ever-ballooning deficits and debts under Modern Monetary Theory (MMT), together with the spread of Central Bank Digital Currencies (CBDC) - national currencies going digital - will accelerate the death of the dollar.

The problem is this spiraling debt bomb is unsustainable. It will never be repaid, at least not in a currency that maintains some semblance of its purchasing power.

By printing so much money in such a short time, the Fed and other central banks are rapidly and dramatically devaluing their currencies.

Even the once-mighty US dollar will be dramatically devalued.

But with every crisis comes opportunity. You see, in times of chaos and uncertainty like the ones I've been telling you about here, precious metals thrive.

In the wake of the COVID-19 shock, gold gained 38% in just six months, setting a record high above $2,000.

More impressively, silver gained 152% during that same period.

It outperformed gold by four times …

That's the story I want to share in this book. It's a story we've seen before. And it's a story we'll absolutely be seeing again.

And again.

And again.

More crises will come our way. And tucked within each of those coming crises will be opportunities to make big money with silver.

Want additional proof?

In the 1970s, economic conditions were like what we're seeing today - high inflation caused by big money printing.

The U.S. money supply multiplied, causing the dollar to lose two-thirds of its purchasing power in that decade alone.

Commodity investments gained wildly over stocks as they followed inflation higher.

Interest rates reached an all-time high of 20% in 1980, and mortgages touched 18%.

It was all triggered by a major reset of the global financial system. In 1971, U.S. President Richard Nixon cut the U.S. dollar's tie to gold.

Inflation was causing money to lose purchasing power. It took more dollars to buy the same basket of "stuff."

That led to a massive transfer of wealth as inflation soared, the stock market stumbled, and bond prices crashed.

The winners were the folks who invested in commodities and precious metals like silver.

Indeed, silver was the big standout. Between 1971 and 1980, silver prices gained an incredible 3,700%, while gold gained a very hefty 1,400%.

When silver starts to outpace gold, as it did again recently, it signals that we're in the second half of a precious metals bull market.

Inflation is hitting 40-year highs. Deficits and debt have exploded in recent decades. And they multiplied even further in the last couple of years thanks to the COVID-19 pandemic.

Global debts and money-printing are devaluing currencies at an accelerating pace. It won't be long before we reach an epic new crisis.

That's why we now have ideal conditions for *The Great Silver Bull*.

I just can't overstate the enormous potential this opportunity offers.

This is going to be **the largest silver bull market we've ever experienced,** bigger even than the crazy 1970s.

That's because **we are barreling towards another global financial reset** – one that dwarfs the one we saw when the U.S. dollar was cut loose from gold.

This time the current debt situation is four times worse.

And it will lead to the biggest transfer of wealth in history.

Most people will be caught off-guard. Today they have nearly all their financial wealth in ETFs, mutual funds, stocks, and bonds - sectors that will get *crushed* in the next bear market.

You don't have to be one of the victims. You don't have to get swindled out of a comfortable retirement.

The big winners - and maybe the **only** winners - will be the folks who stake their futures on alternatives like precious metals ... and especially silver.

That's exactly what happened during the 2008 Financial Crisis. Some fund managers foresaw it, so they positioned their investments years in advance and profited handsomely.

Silver and gold excelled. The gold price doubled, while the silver price tripled between 2008 and 2011.

We're going to see this again.

That's the view of the future I'm going to share. That's the investing blueprint that I'm going to *give* to you.

Why I Wrote *The Great Silver Bull*

Silver is a "must-own" investment for folks who want to survive what's headed our way.

It has proven itself as a superb inflation hedge and store of value for thousands of years. It's also great insurance against chaos and uncertainty.

Central banks create money with no effort. A few keystrokes on their computers generate billions of dollars within seconds. They don't consult or even warn people using that currency to store their life savings.

By contrast, creating silver demands a lot of effort. And its supply is very limited. That makes silver the ultimate protection against governments as they continuously inflate the money supply to 'paper over' their ongoing mistakes.

Unfortunately, most investors only wake up to silver's potential after it has already soared in price and made the big headlines. They'll rush in late - creating massive windfalls for the folks who invested first.

Folks like you.

Silver is your opportunity.

It's your chance to protect and grow your wealth and to set you up for financial freedom.

The great thing is, it's still early days in this silver bull market.

I've been following, writing about, and investing in precious metals (and especially silver) for more than two decades. So, I can say with complete confidence that I've *never* seen a better setup for silver and silver stocks to soar than the one we have right now.

Over the last 15 years, I've been editing financial newsletters covering countless silver investments. I've visited mines and met with management to size up opportunities. My extensive network of contacts, built up over the years, gives me access to the top industry insiders.

As a silver expert, I've presented at numerous conventions and hosted investment discussion panels. I've been interviewed by - or written for - such institutions as **Forbes**, **Kitco**, **BNN Bloomberg**, **The Financial Post**, **Seeking Alpha,** and others.

After the coronavirus panic, I saw silver scream higher and outpace even gold. That's when I decided to share my knowledge about silver investing.

So, I launched a specialized silver newsletter: **Silver Stock Investor** (silverstockinvestor.com), to bring my best real-time ideas to subscribers. **Silver Stock Investor** is all about what I buy and sell to profit from silver.

But I wanted to catalogue my newest predictions - and the system for cashing in on them - in one place.

That's why I wrote *The Great Silver Bull*.

I want this book to be a true game-changer for you.

The Great Silver Bull is your personal blueprint for what I see as a once-in-a-generation silver opportunity.

This book tells you all you need to know, from silver's crucial role through history to the way you can build and manage your own silver investment portfolio.

And it does so in five easy-to-read, easy-to-act-upon parts.

In **Part I - A Brief History of Silver**, I'll show you the great reasons silver, not gold, became the first truly international currency - and the unique properties that make it an ideal form of money.

Today, central banks and governments reject it because it limits their ability to print endless amounts of currency. That's why silver, like gold, was removed from our money over 50 years ago. But roughly every hundred years or so, the world's reserve currency loses its status. And that causes financial upheaval, igniting silver's value. You'll even see how Berkshire Hathaway, the company run by legendary billionaire investor Warren Buffett, earned about $100 million from silver.

In **Part II - Why Silver Matters Today**, I'll explain what central planners, past and present, have done to the money supply. You'll learn about why that always ends badly for investors who don't see it coming. I will highlight all the tricks and strategies central planners have used, and continue to use, to try and climb their way out of huge debts. Spoiler alert: It's not good for the little guy.

I will also describe the secret key to knowing when conditions are "right" - meaning they practically guarantee that silver prices will rise. It's a little-known indicator that reflects the interaction between inflation and interest rates. And you'll see how it can help you profit from silver.

In **Part III - Silver: The Irreplaceable Metal**, you'll learn why silver is unique as both a monetary and industrial metal. And being the most reflective and conductive, silver is an irreplaceable metal in countless applications. Mother Nature even gave silver a quirky supply profile that makes it resist the normal laws of economics.

Silver already holds a crucial role in solar panels, electronics, telecommunications, medicine, and electric vehicles. But the global push against climate change emphasizes renewable energies and electrification. What's more, in reaction to the COVID-19 pandemic, governments launched massive infrastructure spending programs that favour a "green economy." And that's igniting silver demand like never before - creating an ideal scenario for you to make huge gains from silver investments.

My research also led me to make an interesting connection between silver and cryptocurrencies. You see, people will eventually lose faith in their money, triggering a global financial reset. They will look for a new form of money that has cryptocurrency's convenience and is backed by an underlying commodity. I think silver could play a vital role in a new digital currency that also has intrinsic value.

But here's the crucial point for you to understand. All these monetary and industrial silver drivers have come together, at the same time, like never before. That makes for amazing opportunities to profit from silver, which tends to enjoy massive multi-year bull markets.

In **Part IV - Silver: Unique and Set to Soar**, you'll see that there are distinct factors that drive silver and silver investments. For example, the silver market is just one-tenth the size of the gold market, so it takes much less buying pressure to send silver prices sky high. What's more, social media has dramatically highlighted the silver opportunity and rallied silver enthusiasts, introducing it to a whole new generation of investors. These aspects will help drive silver to new record highs - far more than even the most-bullish scenarios. To give you confidence in my prediction, I'll show you five different ways I arrive at the same peak target price for silver.

But, most importantly, in **Part V - Investing in Silver: The Ultimate Guide**, you'll learn all about the different silver investment options available, from coins and bars to junior exploration stocks, and everything in between. I've invested in all of these. So, I'll share my insights and what I see as **the ideal way** to build a silver investment portfolio. I'll also give you **my five secrets to managing risk**.

You see, silver goes through multi-year bull markets when it soars by thousands of percent. And silver stocks leverage those gains, generating returns that can reach tens of thousands of percent.

Still, all great bull markets come to an end. *The Great Silver Bull* will too. That's why you'll get my four clues that will tell you when that day comes - when silver is approaching its peak. That won't come for years - but, after all, you'll want to maximize your gains by selling your silver investments when the silver bull market *eventually* comes to an end.

By the end of this book, you'll know more about silver than 99.9% of investors. You'll know more than your friends and colleagues. You'll even know more than most of the so-called "experts."

It doesn't matter whether you're an individual investor managing your own account - or an investment pro running money for others - my goal is for you to understand the silver opportunity and to find the best ways to profit.

The bottom line: This is destined to become the biggest silver bull market we've ever seen.

I'm here to guide you.

And I'm thrilled that you took this important step for your financial future.

Part I:
A Brief History of Silver

Introduction: The Silver (R)Evolution

Money is the greatest invention in history.

That's a bold statement, I know.

Bold … but accurate.

After all, what about agriculture, transportation, the printing press, medicine, airplanes, or computers? Aren't they greater?

They're great innovations, to be sure. But none of these would be possible if people couldn't engage in "transactions." Our ability to exchange goods and services with each other has allowed for astounding human progress.

Barter came first, but that was complicated and not very convenient.

Once discovered, silver quickly became a store of value, making trade a lot easier. Commerce allowed societies to grow and prosper.

It was no accident. Silver has properties that, like gold, make it an ideal form of money.

Silver coins became the first truly international currency, helping people of different nations and cultures trade with each other. This metal remained a reliable form of money for millennia - outlasting empires, dynasties, and wars.

It's only been in the last 50 years that we've seen the world abandon precious metals as a basis for currency. I'll show you how, throughout history, debasing currencies or using unbacked paper - also called fiat money - often led to the collapse of empires that had lasted for centuries.

Today's ever-growing supply of unbacked money is a frightening repeat of history. We'll have a closer look at this in **Part II**.

In the last hundred years, we've seen several crucial events in the realm of fiat currencies.

These were triggered by monetary and/or geopolitical decisions that favoured the state, but not necessarily its citizens. Those with the foresight to have been invested in silver managed to shelter their assets and thrive.

I will detail some of these events to help you prepare and sidestep similar risks in the future.

Chapter 1: Silver as Money Through History

Exactly when silver first appeared as money, as we understand it, is a matter of great debate.

But its influence is undeniable. To this day, in more than 14 languages, the word "silver" means money. The country of Argentina got its name from the Latin "argentum," or "silver," first used by the Spanish and Portuguese conquistadors who voyaged along the Río de la Plata ("River of Silver") in the early 16th century.

As you'll see, silver's been part of daily life for more than 5,000 years. I'll take you from that metal's origins as money all the way through to a few decades ago, when it was completely removed from our coinage.

Silver has been used by every major empire, starting with ancient Greeks up to 20th century America.

Later, I'll show you how I believe that silver will return to form a basis for money once again. But first, let's explore the past to better understand where we are headed.

We know silver was used going back as far as 5,000 years. By 2,000 BC, Babylonia, a state in ancient Mesopotamia (in modern-day Iraq), had become a developed society. It had a sophisticated system of credit and money, which included both barley and silver. These two commodities formed a dual monetary system, helping to exchange goods and create a standard of value. A legal ratio of 180 grains of barley to an equal weight in silver was a "shekel." Silver gradually became more dominant than barley.

Sometime around 800 BC, it appears the Greeks fashioned the first coins. The earliest ever were found in the Temple of Artemis at Ephesus (modern-day Turkey). These were oval shaped Lydian coins made of electrum, a naturally occurring alloy of gold and silver.

But it was a silver coin, the Athenian drachma, that stood the test of time and soon became the world's first international currency.

For 300 years, from the time of Solon around 600 BC until Alexander the Great around 300 BC, the drachma maintained its weight of 67 grains. Alexander ultimately introduced the drachma to India and, from there, it spread further east.

Rome eventually absorbed a declining Greece into its empire. But during 600 years of Greek dominance, the drachma only dropped from 67 to 65 grains. That was an astounding accomplishment for an international currency because few others have lasted beyond a hundred years before being replaced. Personal liberty allowed the economy to thrive. The drachma flourished as it remained highly valued.

But Rome didn't share Greece's monetary discipline. As a result, it became a case study of widespread currency devaluation and the first example of a slow-motion financial crisis in monetary history.

Its currency, the denarius, was introduced in 277 BC. The denarius, modelled after the Greek drachma, was established at nearly the same weight and size. Although it weighed 66 grains at inception, the denarius had lost a modest 6 grains (or 9%) in its first 250 years, until the time of Christ.

Sadly, for the Romans, things declined rapidly from there. Rome's thirst for expansion and military dominance led to a swift debasement of the currency; some of the silver content was replaced with cheaper metals. The empire was plagued by a continuous stream of threats and problems, including a high dependence on imports, wars on several borders, and revolts by slaves and peasants.

The response, which set the stage for the similar monetary tactics of today, was to mint more currency of lesser value. In 64 AD, Emperor Nero introduced a lighter silver coin that contained 10% copper and was instantly worth 25% less than its predecessor. Economic scholars widely believe the fall of Rome was precipitated by ongoing currency debasement and inflation.

And yet, other empires used silver to accumulate wealth during overlapping periods of history.

Silver ingots were used in China as a medium of exchange as far back as the Han dynasty, from 206 BC - 220 AD. That lasted nearly 1,000 years, but the silver ingots were mainly a store of wealth until the start of the Song dynasty in the year 960.

Then something revolutionary happened in the world of currency.

During the Song Dynasty (960 - 1279), copper alloy coins and silver were still in use. But, as of 1024, the government became the only entity to issue paper currency. Marco Polo marveled at this, saying: "Everybody takes them readily, for wheresoever a person may go throughout the Great Kaan's dominions he shall find these pieces of paper current and shall be able to transact all sales and purchases of goods by means of them just as well as if they were coins of pure gold."

Over the next few centuries, Imperial China alternated between banning silver in favour of paper money, which would depreciate, and lifting the ban to allow silver usage.

The Middle East also came to appreciate and prosper by using silver as money.

The dirham is a silver coin in the Islamic world, deriving its name from the Greek drachma. Its use has also spanned centuries.

Ultimately, both the Byzantine Empire and Europe would use it.

In late Antiquity and the early Middle Ages, the Frankish Empire dominated Western Europe and used the denarius under Charlemagne. Great Britain's use of silver coins dates back to around 775, when 240 silver pennies were equal to one pound of silver, which eventually became the pound sterling. These pennies were fashioned after Charlemagne's denarius.

By the early 1500s, Spain and Portugal had begun tapping rich sources of silver in the New World, especially Bolivia, Peru and Mexico. The Cerro Rico, or "rich hill" in Potosí, Bolivia, is said to have produced 45,000 tons of silver for Spain between 1556 and 1783.

In 1515, mines in Joachimsthal, Bohemia (today in the Czech Republic, then in Germany) supplied the silver to mint coins called Joachimsthaler. That name would eventually be shortened to just "thaler." As those coins spread across Europe, thaler morphed into the English word "dollar."

In 1785, the United States brought in a silver standard modeled on the Spanish milled dollar. Through the Coinage Act of 1792, America made the dollar its official currency. Although silver and gold coins were legal tender, the massive debts that financed the Revolutionary War saw silver coins hoarded as U.S. President Thomas Jefferson suspended their minting in 1806.

Silver dollars would circulate over the next 150 years, but a shortage of coins and silver ultimately led to the 1965 Coinage Act. This act eliminated all silver from coinage other than silver half dollars. Naturally, most silver-containing coins gradually disappeared from circulation as people hoarded them for their inherent value. This phenomenon is known as Gresham's Law: bad money drives out good. Today, people still search out circulated pre-1964 coins (ironically called "junk silver") for their silver content.

As you can see, silver has endured for thousands of years, outlasted empires, and resisted political bungling. That's because it has intrinsic value, something that's not about to change.

Key Takeaways

- Silver has been used as money for more than 5,000 years.
- Debased money led to the end of empires.
- Silver was part of modern money until the 1960s.

Chapter 2: Global Reserve Currencies

As a kid, I wanted to be an archaeologist.

I was captivated by ancient Egypt's pyramids, pharaohs, and military dominance. Indeed, I still feel that way - and who could blame me: Egypt is considered one of the oldest and most culturally rich civilizations in history.

My fascination with Egypt led me to a crucial lesson - one that I continue to benefit from today, and that I'm now passing along to you.

Over the centuries, world powers come and go, and different regions each get their turn. But when a country or its empire becomes dominant, usually through economic and military might, its currency does, too.

And it's the currency story we want to zero in on.

Let's start by talking about a "reserve currency."

A reserve currency is one that's commonly used in international trade. In the past century, it's also been the currencies central banks own as part of their foreign-exchange reserves.

(Later on, I'll show you how you can use silver to become your own, independent central bank. That will help you become less reliant on the current banking system - a move that will allow you to better control your own financial destiny ... no matter what's happening on the global financial stage.)

Over the past 600 years, a string of currencies has achieved global reserve status, with one giving way to another. This chart shows that each has "owned" this spot for about a century.

Global Reserve Currencies since 1450

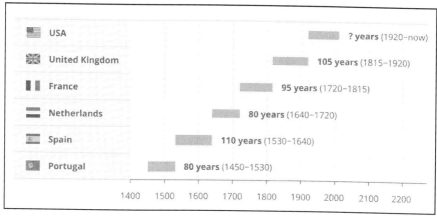

Source: cointelegraph.com

Silver and/or gold backed each of the currencies in the chart above.

Starting in 1878, the U.S. government issued "silver certificates," which were legal tender in the form of paper. They looked like today's paper money but represented a specific amount of silver bullion. This allowed people to own physical silver without taking possession. Notice how at the very top it says, "Silver Certificate."

U.S. Silver Dollar Certificate, 1935

Source: picryl.com (public domain)

The U.S. dollar was partially backed by gold until Aug. 15, 1971. That's when, in response to spiraling inflation, U.S. President Richard Nixon suspended international convertibility of the greenback to gold - a move that set the stage for the highly inflationary 1970s.

Today the world operates on a fiat standard.

Fiat money is government-issued currency backed by nothing more than the "full faith and credit" of the government.

According to the U.S. Treasury itself:

> *"Federal Reserve notes are not redeemable in gold, silver, or any other commodity, and receive no backing by anything. This has been the case since 1933. The notes have no value for themselves, but for what they will buy."*

There are no real limits to printing fiat currency, and that always leads to oversupply and inflation. Ultimately, every fiat currency has a limited life span, and eventually fails.

Because the greenback is currently the global reserve currency, commodities like oil, metals and grains are priced in U.S. dollars. As a result, countries must hold large quantities of dollars to pay for resources. The dollar has become the world's de facto reserve currency. But because the dollar is an unbacked fiat currency, we've essentially been living in a real-world "experiment" for the past 50 years.

At this point, as the chart I showed you suggests, the U.S. dollar has already overstayed its welcome.

IMFBlog says that, as of late 2020, the greenback's share of central bank reserves had fallen to 59%. That's a 25-year low, according to the International Monetary Fund's (IMF) Currency

Composition of Official Foreign Exchange Reserves (COFER) survey.

And it's about to get worse for the dollar.

As other world powers look to dethrone the dollar's dominance, the euro and the Chinese renminbi (yuan) have gained importance.

This view is supported by Russia saying it will sell all U.S. dollar assets from its National Wealth Fund, favouring the euro, Chinese yuan, and gold instead. China has also been on a steady path of shrinking its $1 trillion in U.S. Treasury bond holdings.

All of this accelerated in February 2022 when Russia invaded and attacked neighboring Ukraine.

Hesitant to put soldiers on the ground, much of the West quickly retaliated against Russia through *financial warfare*. The biggest impact came from heavy sanctions, like cutting Russia off from global trade and the SWIFT global interbank payments system, used by nearly all financial institutions.

Within just four days Russian interest rates doubled from 9.5% to 20%. The Russian ruble currency turned to rubble, losing 30% in one day, and half its value against the US dollar within a month. There was a run on Russian banks, as people clamored to withdraw cash. Automated teller machines (ATMs) faced long queues and quickly ran empty.

Russia has been buying domestic miners' gold production for years to bolster its war chest. That helped triple the country's official stash to 2,300 tonnes of gold - the world's 5th largest holdings - representing 20% of total national reserves. When the ruble crashed, the government abolished a value-added tax on gold and silver, triggering a race by households to buy physical metals. That caused the central bank to halt its gold purchases

28

to ease supply and meet household demand. In effect, Russians were buying gold and silver to preserve their wealth while the ruble fell to historic lows.

Within days gold soared, challenging its August 2020 high of $2,070, while silver spiked to $27.

But there were other unintended consequences.

As Ken Griffin, CEO of hedge fund Citadel put it, the sanctions effectively "weaponized the dollar". He continued:

> *"The U.S. dollar is the reserve currency for the world. That's an incredible asset for our nation, particularly as our nation faces record levels of indebtedness.*
>
> *When we put on the table that your dollars will be seized or you can't move dollars, we are telling the rest of the world to embrace other currencies in their portfolio, and we diminish the value of the dollar as the world's currency. American taxpayers are going to pay for this in the form or higher interest rates on our debt. It hurts our country in a profound way."*

Just three weeks after punishing financial sanctions were imposed on Russia, Saudi Arabia accelerated talks to price some of its oil sales to China in yuan, further hindering the US dollar's dominance.

When a society loses confidence in its currency, as has happened countless times throughout history, it can no longer function properly. The currency's ability to store value falls because it's printed at such a rapid rate.

People lose trust and no longer want to hold cash. Some of the most glaring examples from the past century are the hyperinflations of Weimar Germany, Zimbabwe, Argentina and - more recently - Venezuela. In the 1990s, Yugoslavia endured inflation of 300 million percent per month.

This will happen again, so you must be ready. Preparation is critical. Anyone who owned enough silver through the hyperinflations of the past 100 years managed to survive and protect their finances.

Remember, silver has had a long and proven history of backing paper money - and serving as money itself.

Now let's look at why a silver standard made so much sense.

Key Takeaways

- Global reserve currencies are used in international trade and held by central banks.
- In the past 600 years each reserve currency has lasted about a century, with each backed by silver and/or gold.
- The U.S. dollar as the world's unbacked reserve currency is a failing experiment.

Chapter 3: Silver is Ideal Money

For thousands of years, silver has proven itself to be a superior form of money.

Like gold, it has the most suitable characteristics.

There are five basic reasons that's true. But I'll show you eight additional features that make it so ideal.

Greek philosopher Aristotle (384-322 BC) laid out the five main principles. You'll see, it's not a coincidence that his Greek predecessors had already been using silver as money for centuries.

The five reasons silver is the king currency:

1. **Silver is durable:** It won't go rancid like wheat or barley, and it won't fall apart from handling it.

2. **Silver is divisible:** You can separate it and recombine it, all without affecting its value or properties. That makes it particularly easy to accept as payment in one place and offer it in another. (The Spanish silver dollar was the original basis for the U.S. dollar, and it was worth eight Spanish reales. That's why it was known as "pieces of eight.")

3. **Silver is convenient:** That's because it has considerable value, so you can pay for many things without having to carry around an excessive amount.

4. **Silver is consistent:** Every piece of silver, large or small, has the same properties as every other. When melted down, they are indistinguishable.

5. **Silver has intrinsic value:** That means it can be used in

other applications, like in industry, so it has a "real" worth. And since there's plenty of work required to find and extract it from the earth, silver will always have value.

Beyond this, other aspects of silver make it particularly attractive as money.

Silver can't be printed: When it backs a currency, that limits how much a government can print, avoiding runaway inflation.

Silver is nearly indestructible: At worst, it will tarnish. Silver jewelry and coins made thousands of years ago are regularly discovered by archaeologists and treasure hunters. Some are even found by accident, like when farmers turn over their land. In short, unless you lose or sell it, your silver is not going anywhere.

Silver has no counterparty risk: Unlike a bond or stock, you don't depend on someone else to honor it. There's no chance of default.

Silver is private: A few ounces give you direct, discrete control over an asset that is valuable.

Silver is liquid: You can sell your silver almost anywhere, anytime. It has often been a lifesaver for displaced people.

Silver can't be hacked: It's not just digits in a database somewhere for you to depend on. And it doesn't rely on electricity or the internet to be accessible.

Silver holds its value: Of course, over time, that will fluctuate. But over years and decades, and especially compared to fiat money, silver always wins out.

Naturally, central planners know very well that precious metals make for the best money. That's why most central bank vaults hold thousands of tons of gold as reserves.

The United States holds more than 8,000 metric tons, Germany has some 3,300 metric tons, and Italy and France each store about 2,400 metric tons.

But those central bankers also know that backing their currencies with silver or gold runs counter to Modern Monetary Theory (an economic concept I'll explain later) - and their ability to print currency at will for their favourite programs and projects. In short, tying their currency to precious metals is their biggest nemesis.

An unbacked fiat currency system faces no such limits. Throughout history, many have sought control of the money supply. Essentially, it gives them power over a country's treasury and credit, and by extension power over the nation.

In the early 1800s, Nathan Mayer Rothschild of the Rothschild banking family famously said: "I care not what puppet is placed upon the throne of England to rule the Empire on which the sun never sets. The man who controls Britain's money supply controls the British Empire, and I control the British money supply."

Now I'm going to explore with you a few important 20th century events. These show just how precious metals caused grief for the leaders at the time.

The bottom line: gold and silver were rejected because they restricted government spending.

Key Takeaways

- Greek philosopher Aristotle stated five main rules why silver and gold are ideal money.
- Central banks own thousands of tons of gold reserves.

- Central planners reject precious metals as money because they limit their influence and control.

Chapter 4: The Great Silver Heist

In the past, governments have at times outlawed the ownership of silver and gold which backed currencies.

The risk of a similar event today is minimal because these metals are no longer used to provide value to any currency.

The Federal Reserve Act of 1913 required the U.S. dollar (Federal Reserve Notes) be 40% backed by gold. But by the late 1920s, the U.S. Federal Reserve was already bumping up against its credit limit. Most economists and financial historians now believe this limit exacerbated the October 1929 stock market crash - and the ruinous Great Depression that followed.

At the time, the gold price was fixed at $20.67 per ounce. In 1933 the U.S. money supply was limited by the "gold standard" - while the economy was mired in a severe depression. So, on April 5, 1933, President Franklin D. Roosevelt signed Executive Order 6102 into law.

The order outlawed the "hoarding" of gold coins, gold bullion, and gold certificates within the continental United States. The rationale was that it was delaying economic growth and worsening the depression. In other words, the government made it largely illegal for people to own physical gold.

Citizens were required to turn in all but a small number of their gold coins, bullion, and certificates to the Federal Reserve by May 1, 1933, in return for $20.67 per ounce. They were still allowed to own up to $100 in gold coins, or about five troy ounces. Collectible (numismatic) coins and gold used in industry, art, or professions such as by dentists, jewelers, and artists were exempt.

On Jan. 30, 1934, the Gold Reserve Act mandated that all gold and gold certificates held by the Federal Reserve were to be transferred and titled to the U.S. Treasury and barred the Treasury and other financial institutions from exchanging dollar bills for physical gold.

President Roosevelt then immediately raised the fixed legal price of gold from $20.67 to $35, effectively devaluing the dollar by 69%. This act instantly wiped out nearly 70% of Americans' dollar-denominated savings. It paved the way for a large increase in the money supply, and therefore inflation, in the hopes of lifting the nation out of its deflationary depression. It also incentivized the world's gold miners to increase production while foreigners exported their gold to the United States, helping to further increase the nation's reserves.

Much less known, however, is President Roosevelt's 1934 Executive Order 6814.

It's an order that I refer to as *The Great Silver Heist.*

And with good reason.

While Executive Order 6102 focused on gold, Order 6814 nationalized all privately owned silver bullion and domestically mined silver.

Privately owned silver bullion had to be turned in to U.S. Mints and was purchased at 50 cents per ounce, while the government paid 64 cents an ounce for domestically mined silver.

Americans turned in 109 million ounces within the 90-day deadline. The order specifically excluded nationalizing 90% silver (content) coins because the goal was to use the acquired silver to increase coinage in circulation - part of the money supply.

When the president made gold ownership illegal and devalued the dollar by 69%, the United States was suddenly on a de facto silver standard - until 1944.

That's when the Bretton Woods Agreement established the dollar as the world's gold-backed reserve currency. And that brought an end to the silver standard in America.

But the U.S. gold standard would last only 27 years.

Key Takeaways

- Gold ownership in the U.S. became illegal in 1933 so more dollars could be printed.

- That devalued the U.S. dollar overnight by 69%, wiping out huge wealth for citizens.

- Privately owned silver was nationalized in 1934 to increase silver coinage supply.

Chapter 5: The Nixon Shock
(aka The Death of the "Gold Standard")

Wars are messy.

That's not only true as they're unfolding. What follows can also change the course of history.

After World War I, the Treaty of Versailles transferred massive British and French debts onto Germany. Unable to fully repay, Germany just kept printing unbacked money, leading to hyperinflation. Anyone holding a modest amount of silver through that period was protected from huge financial losses.

Unbending creditor nations insisted on repayment of Allied war debts, which led to a failure of the international financial system, finally causing a global depression. That would sow the seeds for World War II.

In 1944, World War II still had a year to go. But two world wars in just 25 years was almost too much for the global economy to bear. The political and economic strains were triggers. Bretton Woods' planners wanted to avoid the fallout caused by the Treaty of Versailles. The goal was to manage currencies and commerce mainly between the United States, Canada, Australia, Western Europe, and Japan.

The most important result of Bretton Woods was that participating nations had to establish monetary policy maintaining fixed exchange rates between their currency and a reserve currency, the U.S. dollar, which itself was convertible to gold at $35 per ounce.

Foreign governments and their central banks were then able to exchange dollars for gold from the US upon request. This made the U.S. dollar "as good as gold." In effect, it led to the dollar becoming the world's reserve currency, with most international transactions being concluded in the greenback.

But America soon embarked on costly wars in Korea and, later, Vietnam.

President Lyndon B. Johnson rejected taxation to pay for Vietnam War expenditures. So, the U.S.'s positive trade balance quickly dropped as dollars flowed out to pay for military spending, and inflation soared.

Foreign-dollar holders quickly saw the currency was losing its purchasing power. The French coined the term "America's exorbitant privilege," referring to the U.S. dollar's benefits as the world's reserve currency. In 1965, French President Charles de Gaulle sent the French Navy to America to collect gold in exchange for its U.S. dollar reserves. Many others quickly followed.

Sensing an impending crisis, President Nixon "closed the gold window" on Aug. 15, 1971, to end the outflow of gold. He suspended convertibility of the US dollar into gold.

That ended a vital feature of the Bretton Woods system, and it quickly fell apart. Currencies were soon allowed to float at fluctuating market-exchange rates. With the dollar no longer tied to gold, the United States was free to print and inflate its money supply unrestricted.

It was only in 1974 that Americans could once again own gold. President Gerald Ford removed the restriction when he signed a bill to "permit United States citizens to purchase, hold, sell, or otherwise deal with gold in the United States or abroad."

During the 1970s the dollar, then completely detached from gold, went on to lose two thirds of its purchasing power. The price of gold rose about 1,400%. And the price of silver went up an astounding 3,700%.

That was driven, at least in part, by an infamous attempt to corner the silver market.

Key Takeaways

- Unbacked currencies allow politicians to pursue big spending and military conflict.

- Nations print fiat currency to repay debts, leading to hyperinflationary collapses.

- U.S. President Nixon cut the dollar's tie to gold, triggering big inflation in the 1970s.

Chapter 6: Silver Squeeze 1.0

In 1974, oil tycoon H.L. Hunt died, leaving behind billions.

At the time, his sons Herbert and Nelson "Bunker" Hunt understood that investors would seek shelter from inflation by buying silver and gold.

They certainly got that right.

So, the two brothers plowed their inheritance into the commodities market, buying up physical silver reserves and even futures contracts. But rather than settling those contracts in cash as they expired, the brothers would take delivery of physical silver. They rapidly built a massive silver stockpile and kept using their money to acquire more.

Eventually, they would lean on the family reputation, borrowing against their fortune in the process. Herbert and Nelson even persuaded other wealthy investors, including those in Saudi Arabia, to accumulate ever more physical silver and buy futures contracts.

Their sizeable silver holdings began pressuring traders and speculators who were short silver. With holdings worth $4.5 billion, the Hunts dominated the silver market, ultimately pushing silver prices to $50 in January 1980. Their actions ignited Washington's ire, which saw this as market manipulation.

Commodities regulators limited the issuance of long silver futures contracts, blocking the Hunts from buying more. That lack of buying opened the door to pressure silver prices downwards through shorting the market. The Hunts felt the growing burden of rising margin calls on their outstanding loans.

Intent on quashing the Hunts' actions, the Federal Reserve asked banks to stop lending for speculation. As the markets realized the Hunts were at risk of default, the silver price accelerated downward. Seven has long been viewed as a "lucky number", but COMEX "Silver Rule 7" drastically limited the purchase of commodities on margin.

This caused the silver price to fall further, and panic struck the market.

Silver fell by half over just four days on spiraling fears the brothers could no longer meet their obligations. Worries swirled that the brokerage firms through which the Hunts had bought futures contracts could fail. That precipitated "Silver Thursday," March 27, 1980, when the Hunts ultimately missed a margin call, and silver fell swiftly to reach below $11.

But big silver purchases would rev up again just 17 years later.

Key Takeaways

- Billionaire Hunt Brothers attempted to corner the silver market in the mid-1970s.
- It worked temporarily, pushing silver prices to $50 in 1980.
- The Federal Reserve pressured banks not to lend for speculation, quashing the Hunts.

Chapter 7: The Buffett Silver Squeeze

Famed investor Warren Buffett is known for many things, one of which is his ongoing public disdain for gold.

Still, that didn't stop his conglomerate, **Berkshire Hathaway (NYSE: BRK:A/BRK.B)**, from investing in one of the world's top gold miners, **Barrick Gold**. In 2020, Berkshire bought up nearly $600 million worth of Barrick shares.

Much less known, though, is Buffett's big investment in silver.

Back in 1997, Berkshire began buying the metal - a lot of it. By 1998 Buffett had accumulated 130 million ounces, nearly 3,500 tons, of which he took delivery in London.

Now, you might think that buying this much silver would look too much like cornering the market, especially since it caused silver lease rates to soar to 75% on an annualized basis. But that didn't seem to be the case for Berkshire.

And ever the wise value investor, Buffett may well have grabbed silver near its lowest inflation-adjusted price ever recorded.

The following chart shows silver-price trends over a 650-year stretch between 1344 and 1998. The metal's price is adjusted for inflation in 1998 dollars.

Inflation-Adjusted Silver Price, 1344-1998 (1998 dollars)

Source: sdbullion.com

What this shows is Buffett's purchases were very near a 650-year low for the silver price. Berkshire then held onto its silver, eventually selling it in early 2006 at nearly double the cost and locking in a cool $100 million in profits.

What's interesting about the timing of Berkshire's sale is how it lines up with another significant event in the modern history of silver.

Despite some heavy resistance an exchange-traded fund (ETF) - the **iShares Silver Trust ETF (NYSE:SLV)** - ultimately got approval for listing on the American Stock Exchange in April 2006. (An ETF is like a stock. The SLV ETF is meant to track the silver price and is backed by silver).

It was the world's first silver ETF, but not before overcoming serious opposition.

The Silver Users Association, established in 1947, really lobbied the U.S. Securities and Exchange Commission (SEC) to not approve the new silver ETF. In a note to the SEC, this trade

44

group of industrial consumers claimed that its members processed "80% of all silver used in the United States." The group said it opposed the creation of a silver ETF "because of the concerns that doing so will require the holding of physical silver in allocated accounts, thus removing large amounts of silver from the market."

Despite the protest, SLV was approved and began trading with 21 million ounces of silver stored in trust. It was massively popular, and within just two weeks, it held 65 million ounces. In August that year, just four months after its birth, SLV had almost 100 million ounces of silver.

Buffet had sold his 130 million silver ounces just months before the world's first silver ETF was launched and quickly accumulated more than 100 million ounces. Did Buffett sell his silver to help fund the SLV ETF? Is that why it was approved by the SEC? We may never really know. But it does beg the question.

Key Takeaways

- Even Warren Buffett has pulled down huge profits from silver.
- He bought 130 million ounces near silver's 650-year inflation-adjusted low.
- That may have supplied the first silver-backed ETF, approved despite big opposition.

In Part I, I've shown you so far that silver has been money for thousands of years and was key in enabling trade. It has many characteristics that make it an ideal form of money.

Silver has also endured some important challenges in the 20th Century. Still, because of an odd bit of financial irony, I'm extremely optimistic on silver's future.

The outlook for America's - and the world's - economy isn't terrific. But the deeper our economic predicament, the more bullish is the outlook for silver.

In Part II, I'm going to show you why - and start laying the groundwork on what you need to do to protect yourself, profit and start building wealth.

Part II:
Why Silver Matters Today

Introduction: Financial Shenanigans

Money is often seen as something mysterious or complex.

Don't be fooled.

Deep discussions about money supply, interest rates, and inflation are often enough to make your eyes roll back in your head.

But understanding money at its most basic level is critical if a comfortable retirement really matters to you.

And really, at its root, it's not complicated.

Think of money as storing the fruits of your effort.

Money is supposed to represent "stored labor," which you access in the future and spend as you need or wish.

But *maintaining the purchasing power of your money* becomes crucial when you intend on using your savings in the future. And it's even more critical when inflation rises well beyond the level of interest.

Currency is meant to be a unit of account, a medium of exchange, and a store of value.

The problem is when a currency isn't backed by something of intrinsic value, it will lose value over time. You really want a currency to be tied to something that has worth; that's taken time and effort to produce. This mismatch just keeps getting worse because the countries that issue fiat money (unbacked currency) tend to produce ever-growing quantities of it.

In the chapters to come, I'll walk you through some of the most egregious financial shenanigans central planners have pulled off in past centuries and more recent years. You'll better understand what they did, the motivation behind it, and why that's bullish for silver going forward.

Being armed with this kind of insight will give you a huge advantage over other investors - and is the key to the windfall profits we're seeking.

Chapter 8: The Money Supply
is Limitless (Not)

Back in 2011 our family vacation included a stop in Venice, Italy.

Of course, we visited the must-see Rialto Bridge, St. Mark's Basilica, and the Piazza San Marco. Already then, my son was a big movie enthusiast. So, we stopped by the church of San Barnaba, the façade of which was used for a library in the film "Indiana Jones and the Last Crusade".

But for me, being an economic history geek, I had to visit the tiny, ornate Church of San Moisè.

This was clearly not a tourist attraction. Once inside, a mass attended by locals was in progress. I waited patiently. Then I approached the priest and asked him where it was. He pointed to the floor behind me.

I realized then that I had walked right over it.

Just inside the massive, centuries-old wooden front doors lies a large, inscribed floor stone. It caps the final resting place for one of history's biggest financial scammers.

John Law was an infamous Scotsman who helped blow up France's economy. (The photo below shows his name inscribed as Joannis Law of Edinburgh).

Tomb of John Law, Scottish Economist
Church of San Moisè, Venice, Italy

Source: silverstockinvestor.com

I'm fascinated by the story of John Law and the Mississippi Bubble, one of the biggest asset bubbles of the modern world. Knowing Law was buried there, I wanted to see the floor stone marking his tomb.

France's King Louis XIV died in 1715, leaving behind a huge national debt after building opulent castles across France using borrowed money. His heir was five-year old Louis XV. So, the Duke of Orleans was appointed Regent advisor to the young boy. The debt was massive - so large, in fact, that revenues wouldn't even cover the interest payments.

In short, France was bankrupt.

That's when, around 1716, the up-to-that-point unknown John Law appeared on the scene.

He proposed a scheme to quickly wipe out France's debt. Law convinced the duke the problem was a lack of money in circulation, which was limited to only silver and gold. Law got permission to set up the central bank - Banque Générale - to issue banknotes. The bank took in silver and gold, and gave depositors paper receipts, guaranteeing they could be exchanged for silver and gold coins. People bought into it, and the banknotes became widely accepted and circulated. But the bank was only partially backed by precious metals, making it a fractional reserve bank.

Law then created the Mississippi Co., whose royal charter gave it exclusive rights to trade with the Louisiana region in the U.S., a French colony at the time. The French had looked on as the rest of Europe enriched itself by trading with the East Indies. So, the Mississippi Co. was hyped to French citizens, who saw it as an opportunity to gain similar riches from the West. The public eagerly bought shares in the company in exchange for their banknotes.

You'll never guess what happened next...

Whenever shares of the Mississippi Co. started to fall, Law would simply print more banknotes. Enough of this additional paper money was used to buy shares, helping prop up their value and the illusion the company was performing well. In fact, Louisiana was little more than swamp land at the time, producing no real revenue. The company was a flop.

Still, Law managed to inflate the Mississippi Bubble by repeatedly printing more fiat money to boost its share price. But some citizens caught wind that the central bank was issuing more banknotes than it had gold and silver to back. That led to an old-fashioned bank run. The Banque Générale couldn't meet demand for withdrawals, collapsing confidence in France's fiat currency.

In January 1720 inflation soared by 23% and kept rising. It was France's financial reset.

Silver and gold immediately returned as standard money. Law was unable to print more banknotes to support buying of shares in the Mississippi Co. It was exposed as a scheme and collapsed. The disgraced Law escaped as riots broke out, eventually landing in Venice where he later died, then was entombed in the Church of San Moisè.

The lesson from these events is how massively over-printed paper currencies eventually collapse. And it happens much more quickly than people expect.

However, anyone who held onto their silver through this fiat money implosion made out just fine.

But you don't have to look all the way back to Rome, or even the 1700s, to see the devastating effects of debasing currencies. We already know that massive money printing in recent years has caused stock markets and real estate to swell, making them look a lot like today's Mississippi Bubble.

And when it pops, you'll want to own silver.

Look at what's happened to the US dollar. It has lost more than 95% of its purchasing power since 1913.

That means $100 from 1913 buys you less than $5 of goods or services today, falling 3.01% per year (compounded) since then.

I've been telling you that silver protects against weakening currencies.

Here's proof.

The average price of silver in 1913 was 60 cents per ounce. Using a $25-an-ounce price today means silver has gained on average 3.52% per year (compounded) over those 109 years.

It's no coincidence that 1913 is when the newly created U.S. Federal Reserve was granted the ability to manage the American money supply. The supposed goal was to keep the U.S. economy operating on an even keel. But, as we'll see, that hasn't always been the case.

Purchasing Power of the U.S. Dollar Since 1913

Source: Federal Reserve Bank of St. Louis

The dollar has been in a nearly constant state of decline as ever more dollars are created. Ironically, the one exception was the Great Depression, from 1929 to 1933, when the dollar's purchasing power increased. It was a period of deflation coupled with a 31% contraction in the money supply. People were seeing their dollars rise in value as prices fell.

It's not by accident that Executive Order 6102 was signed into law in 1933 to kick-start money printing. The Gold Reserve Act set the stage for the Federal Reserve to essentially print money at will.

In the last 20 years alone, we've seen an acceleration of money-printing worldwide.

Growth of Global Money Supply 2000 - 2021

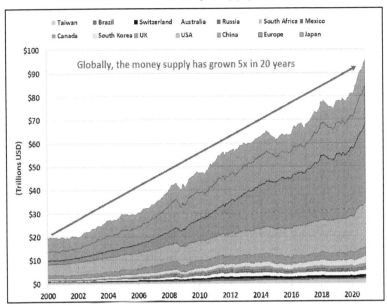

Source: Katusa Research

As the chart shows us, the world's supply of money is up five times in just the last two decades. If you think this looks like a bubble, you're right.

Since then, the U.S. money supply as defined by M2 (cash, checking-and-savings accounts, money-market accounts, and mutual funds) has exploded.

It stood at $4.6 trillion in 2000. By 2021, it reached $19.5 trillion. And it just keeps growing. Even the money-printing response to the 2008 Financial Crisis registers as a minor blip on the following (M2) money-supply chart - a fact that's a real stunner.

US M2 Money Stock 2000 - 2021

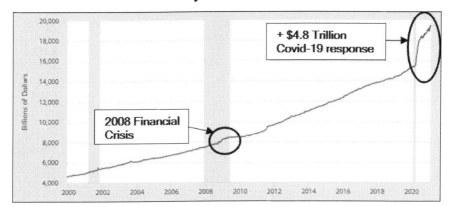

Source: Federal Reserve Bank of St. Louis, silverstockinvestor.com

Here's another stunner - as depicted in the chart above.

By the middle of 2021, in the wake of the COVID-19 pandemic peak, about 25% of all US dollars in circulation had been created in the previous 18 months alone.

Let that sink in for a moment.

The U.S. Federal Reserve's balance sheet doubled in response to the 2008 Financial Crisis from $1 trillion to $2 trillion and kept growing. It reached $4 trillion by 2019, then doubled again to $8 trillion by mid-2021 in response to the COVID-19 pandemic. The Federal Reserve and the federal government pulled out all the stops with massive, unprecedented stimulus spending and economic support for individuals and businesses.

Federal Reserve Total Assets 2003 - 2022

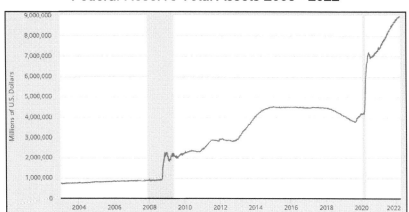

Source: Federal Reserve Bank of St. Louis

This explains why the outstanding federal debt has exploded, from $10 trillion in 2008 to over $30 trillion in 2022.

Let me repeat. **The U.S. debt *tripled* in just 14 years.**

In the 1970s, U.S. federal debt was about 35% of gross domestic product (GDP). Silver enjoyed an enormous bull market in that decade - thanks to strong inflation, which soared to 14.8%.

U.S. Debt to GDP Ratio, 1965 - 2021

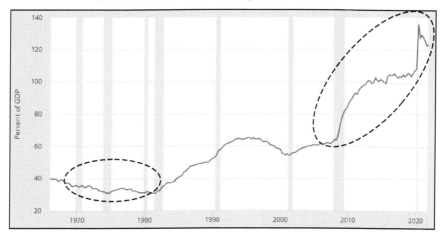

Source: *Federal Reserve Bank of St. Louis, silverstockinvestor.com*

In a move that's become financial-history legend, U.S. Federal Reserve Chair Paul Volcker finally quashed inflation by raising interest rates from 11.2% in 1979 to 20% in 1981. Such sky-high rates, unimaginable today, were possible back then thanks to a much lower national debt level.

Inflation is now returning with a vengeance, but current federal debts have reached 130% of GDP. America owes a lot more money today when compared to its economic output in the 1970s. And that puts its financial stability on a much more precarious footing.

The United States can't afford to significantly raise rates to tame high inflation. With interest rates around 1.4%, the interest costs alone on the debt are about 5% of the national budget. That's forecast to reach 11% of the U.S. federal budget within 10 years, with interest rates at just 2.8%.

According to the Committee for a Responsible Budget, if interest rates gradually rise by just 2% from current levels, Washington will be looking at $11.1 trillion in interest alone over the next decade. Translation: nearly 20% of the current federal budget will go to interest payments.

America - and most of its developed-economy brethren - are in precisely that rickety position. They simply can't afford to raise rates enough if inflation starts to spiral higher. That means higher inflation is less likely to come under control. I expect that will lead to a financial reset, where currencies suffer big losses of buying power.

This wildly accelerating debt spiral is mainly a result of low interest rates. There's not much we can do to prevent that outcome. As I've shown you, that's occurred many times in the past.

Unfortunately, most folks have no clue about what happens when a currency collapses. And they know even less about how to prepare for it. The fact is silver has always protected against these crises.

As you'll see in the next chapter, the experiment with low rates is not new. And it doesn't end well.

Key Takeaways

- Since the Federal Reserve was established in 1913, the dollar is worth 95% less.
- Global money supply has grown five times larger in just the last 20 years, reminiscent of the Mississippi Bubble.
- Huge debts mean we can't afford to raise rates, making higher inflation more likely.

Chapter 9: The Lowest Rates ... Ever

If you don't think we're already at extremes, consider this.

Interest rates are at their lowest levels in 5,000 years of recorded history.

Have a look at the following chart of interest rates, reaching all the way back to 3000 BC.

Interest Rates, 3000 BC to 2000s AD

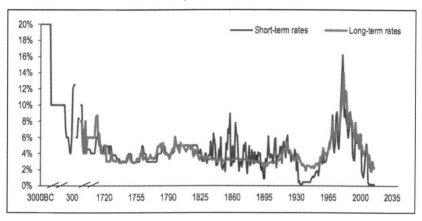

Source: businessinsider.com, Bank of England, Global Financial Data, Home and Sylla, "A History of Interest Rates"

In the *History of Interest Rates*, a seminal work on the subject, author Sydney Homer shows how rates have moved throughout the centuries. He tells us that there have been "repetitious patterns," but also says there has been "a progressive decline in interest rates as the nations or cultures developed and throve, **and then a sharp rise in rates as each 'declined and fell'.**"

I believe we're on the cusp of the U.S. empire's own rapid decline. America's position as the world's leading economy is diminishing. As part of that, Americans will see their standard of living decline.

The middle class will shrink dramatically, widening the gulf between rich and poor. Most advanced economies will suffer from accelerating inflation, a rapidly depreciating currency, and ultimately an inevitable sharp rise in rates. Those viewed as "rich" will be the investors whose holdings include big slices of hard assets - like real estate, commodities, gold, and silver.

Life is about to get a whole lot more expensive.

And if you want proof, look no further back in history than the tough, tough 1970s.

It wasn't disco that "sucked" - it was inflation.

And silver soared thousands of percent in that decade alone.

Coming back to the present day, consider the economic backdrop. The U.S. Federal Reserve's benchmark Federal Funds Rate has been near zero - almost continuously since we exited the Great Financial Crisis in early 2009.

This has never happened before.

Not ever.

And if the lowest interest rates in 5,000 years aren't enough to have you shaking in your shoes, the fact that there's another human intervention layered on this (one that's making things 10 times worse) will certainly do the trick.

___

Key Takeaways

- Interest rates are at their lowest levels in 5,000 years of history.
- After long periods of low rates, they rise sharply, leading to extended economic declines.

- This sets the stage for inflationary shocks, causing silver prices to soar.

Chapter 10: We'll Pay You to Borrow

I'm talking about negative interest rates.

As ridiculous as it may sound, that's when the *borrower is **paid interest*** while the lender is **charged interest**.

Sadly, desperate times led governments and central banks to desperate measures.

A negative-interest rate policy (NIRP) can only happen because central planners intervene and enforce hair-brained ideas. It can't happen naturally. In a free market NIRP shouldn't exist.

Think about it. You're the lender, the one taking on risk by handing your money to a borrower - and you're getting *charged* for doing so. The borrower receives a loan and *gets paid* for it.

This goes against the natural laws of economics. It's completely upside down.

The lender should be rewarded for taking on risk. But we've seen negative rates before and, worryingly, we're seeing them more frequently than ever. After the Great Financial Crisis of 2008 several western nations, mainly in Europe, introduced negative interest rates as a desperate attempt to lift economic growth.

Banks are charged interest on their funds deposited at the central bank to encourage them to lend out instead. Central planners hope negative rates will drive people to invest in the stock market, real estate, and general consumer goods while spurring businesses to spend on expansion, rather than leaving funds idle and being charged for the privilege.

But negative rates are artificial. So, they encourage borrowing and support business ventures that otherwise would not be profitable. When those rates start returning to normal, people go bankrupt, and businesses fail.

As it turns out, this has happened before - back in the 1970s.

Switzerland was the first nation to charge negative interest rates. In the 1970s, its central bank did this to discourage foreign investors from bidding up its currency. The stronger the Swiss franc was, the more costly it became for people holding other currencies to buy Swiss exports.

Notice the timing: the 1970s. Switzerland's economy was geared towards high-value exports, plus it was managed with fiscal responsibility and restraint, making it an attractive safe haven. Before President Nixon slammed shut the gold window, the Swiss franc traded at a fixed exchange rate. Its currency was held artificially low, making its exports relatively cheap and boosting the Swiss economy.

Once the Bretton Woods Agreement ended, currencies began to "float" freely against each other. The Swiss franc more than doubled in value against the US dollar between 1971 and 1978, crushing Swiss exporters.

The Swiss government tried numerous tactics and strategies to discourage foreign deposits and the purchase of Swiss francs, including a 2% quarterly penalty on deposits. That failed, so next came a 12% "negative rate" on non-resident deposits, which worked only temporarily.

Money kept flowing in. By January 1975, after a government emergency meeting, Swiss leaders imposed an astonishing 41% annual penalty on foreign deposits. And still the franc rose against the US dollar.

64

Swiss Franc/U.S. Dollar 1971 - 2011

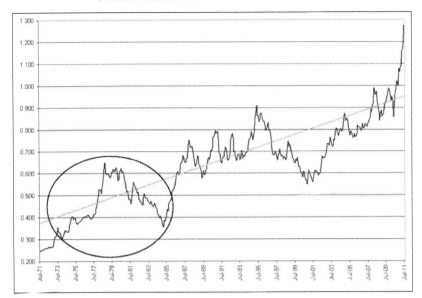

Source: financialsense.com, silverstockinvestor.com

This overwhelmed the Swiss economy, which went into recession as its export sector retreated.

With inflation at just 2.5%, the lowest anywhere, the rest of the world looked on with envy. Their last intervention was to print huge quantities of francs (sound familiar?) to buy other currencies, triggering inflation that eventually could not be tamed.

Once the United States had finally killed its own inflation through massively higher interest rates in the late '70s and early '80s, the Swiss ended this approach as the US dollar rose markedly against the franc.

And yet, just four decades later negative interest rates would come roaring back.

Key Takeaways

- A negative interest rate policy (NIRP) is when lenders are *charged* interest and borrowers are *paid* interest.

- In the 1970s the Swiss were first to use central bank imposed negative interest rates.

- It was a completely ineffective policy, finally righted by the free market.

Chapter 11: Europe's Financial Repression

Four years after the 2008 Financial Crisis, Europe was getting desperate.

Inflation was negligible. Economic growth was anemic. Something had to be done.

Denmark was the first to initiate negative interest rates in 2012. At the time, that turned Danes into the most debt-ridden people in the world.

By 2014 Europe had been plagued with years of falling inflation and stubbornly high unemployment. Inflation had dropped to 0.5%, well below its 2.0% target.

Deflation became the big worry. Unemployment was falling only very slowly and was still high at 11.7%. Youth unemployment levels were at 23.5%. In Greece and Spain, youth unemployment ran at 56.9% and 53.5%, respectively.

Central planners had to act. So, they attempted to employ "unconventional" policies to kick-start the economy. Never mind that it totally failed decades earlier in Switzerland.

The European Central Bank (ECB) announced several measures, but the standout was to lower deposit rates (interest paid to banks on deposits at the ECB) from zero to negative 0.1%. It sounds crazy, but banks suddenly had to pay the ECB to hold their funds.

But it wasn't just bank accounts paying a negative interest rate.

Many government bonds, especially in Europe, were priced to return investors less than their original capital. As ludicrous as this sounds, there are two main reasons why it would happen.

Large investors like multinational corporations, insurance companies, and fund managers often need to park large amounts of cash in safe investment vehicles, and banks only guarantee deposits up to relatively small amounts. Also, speculators may be betting that these bonds will continue to rise in value and pay even lower yields. They buy negative-yielding bonds hoping to resell them later to "the greater fool," pushing yields lower still.

By December 2020, the worldwide total of negative-yielding debt had reached an eye-watering $18 trillion: a new record. That meant fully 27% of the world's investment-grade bonds paid a negative return.

From the onset of the 2020 COVID-19 pandemic, negative rates were not only still in effect, but they were also extended to deal with the new crisis. By mid-2021, many European banks were turning away deposits of 100,000 euros or higher. Even if they accepted them, they were charging 0.5% annually on the funds.

With pandemic lockdowns and uncertainty, people were saving more as they stayed home, plowing their cash into banks. That was the exact opposite of what governments had intended to happen.

Banks were instead encouraging clients to reallocate their funds to other investments. Retirees who had spent decades as frugal savers were being punished, making it impossible for many to live off the interest from their savings.

This phenomenon is known as "financial repression."

It's real. And it's not new. We've been living with these conditions since the Great Financial Crisis of 2008.

Financial repression occurs when governments channel funds away from private sectors to themselves to help reduce debts. They implement policies allowing them to borrow at extremely low rates, funding their spending at low cost. As a result, savers earn returns below inflation rates, which is repressive.

Essentially, people are being pushed towards becoming speculators.

Though a rising stock market is usually seen as reflecting a healthy economy, that's not always true.

With investors watching stock market levels, central planners do everything they can to be supportive. Ultra-low and even negative rates are somewhat effective tools, at least for a while.

From early 2009 to mid-2021, the Dow Jones Industrial Average rose almost fivefold, from 7,000 to 34,000.

Cheap, or nearly-free, money was working.

But central bank-controlled interest rates mean the price to borrow money is set by planners. So, there is no free market in one of the most important markets in the world, the market for money.

And that inevitably leads to big economic extremes, as cheap money pushes market valuations out of whack.

Key Takeaways

- Financial repression is a combination of low interest rates with rising inflation.
- In 2014 Europe imposed negative rates to try and fight persistently low inflation.
- Controlled interest rates mean no free market for money, a crucial global market.

Chapter 12: Pandemic Panic

The COVID-19 pandemic, and worldwide government reactions to it, have been unlike anything we've ever seen.

On March 11, 2020, the World Health Organization (WHO) declared the COVID-19 coronavirus to be a pandemic. Except for health, food and key "essential" services, people around the world were told to stay home. Schools and businesses were shuttered.

Economic activity ground to a sudden, screeching halt on a scale and duration never seen before. It was like the economic world had just stopped turning.

Anyone who could work from home was mandated to do so. Schoolchildren and teachers had to quickly adapt to online learning. Cities and suburbs turned into veritable ghost towns. Many flights, especially international ones, were banned to prevent spreading the virus. People were encouraged to return home from international trips as quickly as possible or risk being stranded for an undetermined period.

Within days governments announced billions of dollars' worth of emergency programs. Those billions quickly turned into trillions. The money was dedicated to pay for medical supplies, compensation for lost income, and to help people and businesses pay their rent or mortgage.

"Stimulus checks" went out to vast numbers of people who were suddenly out of work or were unable to go to work as economic activity dried up. Through no fault of their own, people were being paid to do nothing.

It was a new paradigm - but not a total surprise.

This gave governments cover to kick their use of Modern

Monetary Theory (MMT) into high gear. MMT is a "spend-to-no-end" approach that I'll detail for you later. And it's related to an economic concept known as "helicopter money."

In 1969 famed economist Milton Friedman coined the term "helicopter money" as a way of explaining his notion of "dropping money" from a helicopter to citizens. It was a dramatic suggestion to increase spending and kick-start inflation by having central banks make payments directly to individuals. It was imagined as a boosting strategy, beyond near-zero interest rates, for an economy mired in recession.

In November 2002, then-Federal Reserve Chair Ben Bernanke suggested that helicopter money might help one day to avert deflation - the archenemy of central bankers.

They seek inflation at all costs to ease the burden of government debt repayment. In a deflation scenario, prices fall, and cash rises in value. So, people naturally delay spending and hoard cash as they wait for things to become cheaper still, just like during the Great Depression of 1929 to 1933.

But delayed spending temporarily hurts the economy, potentially leading to recessions. Central bankers hate recessions and think they should do all they can to avoid them, despite being a natural part of economic cycles.

Between 2002 and 2013, well past the 2008 Global Financial Crisis, numerous economists, researchers, and financial leaders had advocated helicopter money as a method of combatting global deflation risks. The appetite for it was limited.

But the next crisis was only a few years away.

Key Takeaways

- The 2020 COVID-19 pandemic lockdowns brought near complete economic shutdown.

- Governments worldwide were desperate to "protect the economy from a crash."

- "Helicopter Money" was used to stimulate spending and kickstart inflation.

Chapter 13: My Financial Epiphany

When the COVID-19 pandemic prompted governments worldwide to provide stimulus checks and massive support to people and businesses, it felt like a financial epiphany.

At least, it did to me.

In the decades I've spent as an analyst, investor and editor specializing in stocks, metals, mining, and economics, I knew that helicopter-money infusions would one day jump from theory to reality.

And because of my studies of Modern Monetary Theory, which I explain in the next chapter, I knew full well the very real and deep-seated problems that new "reality" would bring.

Still, it was shocking to see that day arrive. That's when I realized we were entering a new, accelerated phase towards a reset of the world's financial system.

And the way silver behaved in the following months confirmed once again its role in protecting and growing wealth.

Within a year, the COVID-19 pandemic had stacked an additional $24 trillion to the world's debt pile. The Institute of International Finance estimated half of that increase had come from government-sponsored pandemic-support programs. The world's new dubious debt record reached $289 trillion in the first quarter of 2021. That's 360% of global GDP. And it means central banks have no choice but to try and keep rates generally low to avoid defaults by countries and banks, as well as businesses and people.

This kind of spiraling debt is unsustainable. Such enormous mountains of debt will never be repaid, at least not in a currency that maintains some semblance of its purchasing power.

Governments have three options: repay, default, or inflate.

Repaying would require unpopular cuts to government spending coupled with crippling tax increases. Defaulting, especially for the United States and the most advanced economies, would be a crushing blow to their credibility, shutting them out of credit markets and leading to an enormous financial crisis (yet another one).

That makes inflating the money supply as the most likely scenario since governments get to repay the debt over time with a dramatically depreciated currency. It's easier because this way they repay the debt with dollars that are worth less than when they first borrowed them. Inflation reduces the value of the debt.

The higher inflation is relative to interest rates, the deeper negative rates are. That's what helps large government debtors. But this lethal combination is financial repression against savers.

This reminds me of three quotes that describe in detail our current economic predicament.

The first is from Milton Friedman, the afore-mentioned American economist who received the 1976 Nobel Memorial Prize in Economic Sciences.

> *Inflation is the one form of taxation that can be imposed without legislation.*

The second is from Alan Greenspan, chairman of the U.S. Federal Reserve, from 1987 until 2006.

> *In the absence of the gold standard, there is no way to protect savings from confiscation through inflation. There is no safe store of value.*

The last installment of this trio - and perhaps the most-intriguing of the three - is a comment from the legendary John Maynard Keynes.

Keynes was an English economist, considered one of the most influential economists of the 20th Century. He's responsible for the dominant school of thought today, known as Keynesian economics. Keynes was a big proponent of using fiscal and monetary policies to counter the negative effects of recessions and depression.

> *By a continuing process of inflation, governments can confiscate, secretly and unobserved, an important part of the wealth of their citizens...There is no subtler, no surer means of overturning the existing basis of society than to debauch the currency. The process engages all the hidden forces of economic law on the side of destruction, and does it in a manner which not one man in a million is able to diagnose.*

Over a span of just two decades, we've endured the dot-bomb debacle of 2000, the 2008 Global Financial Crisis, and the 2020 COVID-19 global pandemic - which triggered the fastest stock bear market in modern history.

With each of these disasters, central planners upped the ante, doing the two things they know best:

They kept interest rates down near zero (or negative).

And they printed money like there's no tomorrow.

But there is a tomorrow. There will be a big bill to pay. And silver is the ideal way you can protect yourself from that fallout - and reap windfall profits.

Key Takeaways

- Helicopter Money - really a form of Modern Monetary Theory - was used across developed nations for the first time.

- Governments wanted to avoid deflation and kick-start inflation.

- Helicopter Money worked, but the "genie" was out of the bottle.

Chapter 14: Modern Monetary Theory

*"There is nothing so absurd that it cannot be
believed as truth if repeated often enough."*

WILLIAM JAMES, 19TH-CENTURY
PHILOSOPHER AND PSYCHOLOGIST

I've shown you that an exploding money supply, accelerated by government reactions to the COVID-19 pandemic, will hasten inflation and eat away at your hard-earned savings.

That's bad enough.

But there's another threat. It's a major driver that's gaining traction, and it's going to greatly accelerate the end of the US dollar as the world's reserve currency.

It's called Modern Monetary Theory - better known as MMT. It's an absurd way to manage a nation's finances. But even that is not about to stop its adoption.

I see MMT as the final nail in the dollar's coffin. That's why we need to be on the lookout for the attitudes of governments and central banks towards MMT. It's a perfect fit with the increasingly dominant idea that national debts and deficits don't matter and shouldn't limit government spending.

MMT was first introduced by American economist Warren Mosler in the early 1990s. The internet helped grow exposure and support for the idea.

But I want you to be aware of MMT for two reasons: it's destructive, and it's quickly gaining acceptance.

Here's proof.

In recent years, MMT's biggest proponents have been university finance professors and advisors to U.S. presidential candidates. What's more, in just the first year of the COVID-19 pandemic, *the U.S. Congress committed $5 trillion in fiscal support.*

As a result, **America's national debt exploded by 20% in one year!**

MMT proponents believe governments which print, spend, and borrow in their own fiat currency *should not limit their spending when dealing with economic issues.* They say not to worry, as big spending won't automatically lead to deficits and debt and, even if it does, these don't matter unless they begin generating inflation. Spoiler alert: huge government money-printing in response to COVID-19 pandemic triggered the highest inflation in over 40 years!

Supporters of MMT also tell us that if inflation becomes a concern, governments can just raise taxes to cool spending. But that will only go so far. In practice, raising taxes is always unpopular, and eventually chokes off economic activity.

In fact, most Western nations have already been running their finances on a "limited" model of MMT for a few decades with growing deficits and ballooning debts. Still, for the most part there's been at least some semblance, however meagre, of central bank independence.

But outspoken MMT advocates see the treasury and central bank as one.

They argue the central bank is there to print whatever the government needs, while the treasury's role is to collect taxes and allocate funds to various departments which spend it according to their budgets. Anything needed beyond what's collected in taxes can just be printed into existence. The idea is that governments can't go broke unless they choose to.

But here's a reality check: **this is not how the rest of the world**

works.

A company or an individual can't operate the way MMT says a government should.

First, they don't print their own money and so they don't have that luxury. Second, they can't borrow to infinity because at some point creditors will force them into bankruptcy.

Here's a simple way to wrap your head around the implications of MMT. I compare the U.S.'s finances with a very modest household budget by dropping several zeroes.

U.S. Debt Problem	
U.S. Tax Revenue	$4,060,000,000,000
Federal Budget	$6,900,000,000,000
New Debt	$2,840,000,000,000
National Debt	$30,000,000,000,000
Family Debt Problem	
Annual Income	$40,600
Annual Spend	$69,000
New Credit Card Debt	$28,400
Total Credit Card Debt	$300,000

Source: usdebtclock.org

The family in this case would not stay solvent for long.

MMT economists say that scenario can't happen with a country because it can just keep printing its currency to pay for spending and even to *pay interest on debts* - which is where I think we're headed.

But massive money printing can't go on forever. We know it ends when the public *does* eventually lose confidence in their oversupplied currency.

As I showed you in Chapter 2 Weimar Germany, Yugoslavia, Zimbabwe, Argentina, and Venezuela all learned the hard way that this kind of economic mismanagement leads to hyperinflation and a quick end to their currencies. The difference is none of them were *global reserve currencies*.

The US dollar, however, is. And that makes its demise even more alarming.

Big name economists will tout MMT as a panacea and downplay its flaws and unintended consequences. If you repeat a lie often enough, people will believe it.

Governments will embrace it, salivating at the potential of limitless spending on their favourite pet projects.

Most people, with little understanding, will buy into MMT as a great new economic model that helps get them all the "goodies" governments can promise in return for votes.

Once the MMT genie is let out of its bottle, we can't put it back. Instead, it will run its destructive course. That means a rapid devaluation of the US dollar, and your savings along with it.

Henry Paulson, former US Treasury Secretary during the 2008 financial crisis said, "The United States must maintain an economy that inspires global credibility and confidence. Failure to do so will, over time, put the US dollar's position in peril." Well, at least he got that right.

Don't be fooled. MMT will only exacerbate and accelerate the overspending problems we have today.

Silver remains the ideal hedge against those threats. In Chapter 17 you'll see that's exactly what happened during the high-inflation 1970s, when silver soared and protected those who owned it.

Key Takeaways

- Modern Monetary Theory says nations with their own currency can run large deficits and shouldn't limit government spending.

- Proponents say we can just print the money needed to pay for spending and never have to go broke, but history says otherwise.

- MMT is becoming more popular and will accelerate the demise of the US dollar as the world's reserve currency.

Chapter 15: The Secret Key – Real Rates

Onetime Fed Chair Alan Greenspan understood how crucial it is to own precious metals as insurance against a spendthrift government.

He referred specifically to gold. But as I detailed back in **Part I**, silver has also been "real money" for thousands of years.

As the world was progressively vaccinated and gradually able to exit most limitations of the COVID-19 pandemic, demand for goods and services came roaring back.

But supply-chain disruptions caused severe market dislocations. At the same time, many countries turned inward as they sought to lessen their dependence on foreign supplies - and especially from nations held in a less-than-friendly regard.

This helped kick-start a new commodities super-cycle. A "super-cycle" is when commodities and natural resources like metals, oil, lumber, and agricultural products enter a multi-year phase of consistently escalating demand and prices. A confluence of factors set the stage.

The prior bull market in commodities ran from 2000 to about 2012. That was followed by several years of a severe bear market. Falling prices caused producers to ratchet back their investments in new or existing capacity, a reality that curbed available supply.

But the massive, coordinated global stimulus response to the COVID-19 pandemic launched a new bull market. Average commodities prices doubled in just one year, with some up fourfold and more. This caused fears of inflation, then actual inflation, to return with a vengeance.

And that leads us to the single-best indicator of where precious

metals are headed: real interest rates.

You need to know this - and for one very good reason: Real rates possess an *amazing* predictive capability.

Real rates are simple to understand. They're measured by subtracting inflation (your measure of lost-purchasing power) from current interest rates.

Stated market interest rates may be at 1%. But once you subtract a 4% rate of inflation, your actual return is a minus (negative) 3%. If a bond or certificate of deposit (CD) pays you 1% annually, but inflation is 4%, then you've lost 3%.

That's bad.

Indeed, likes Keynes, the economist once said: "Inflation can confiscate, unobserved, part of your wealth."

When real rates are falling and/or below zero, silver and gold thrive.

This chart compares real rates with the gold price.

10-Year Treasury Constant Maturity Rate vs. Gold Price

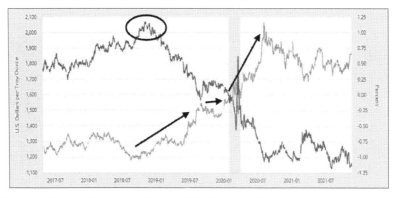

Source: Federal Reserve Bank of St. Louis, silverstockinvestor.com

Real interest rates peaked in late 2018 (red line), and that's when gold began climbing higher (gold line). In late 2019, real rates moved sideways, and gold's climb stalled. But then, in early 2020, sensing the impending pandemic fallout, real rates resumed their fall, and the gold price rallied strongly once again.

As you can see, both price series form an almost-perfect mirror image.

The key takeaway is clear: demand for bonds pushed down their yields, driving negative real rates lower, while demand for gold as a safe haven pushed its price higher.

Gold and silver don't pay interest, but they compete with bonds for investment dollars, which do. However, when real rates are falling or negative, bonds lose that advantage. The "opportunity cost" of holding precious metals disappears.

Now have a look at the same chart, but with silver instead.

10-Year Treasury Constant Maturity Rate vs. Silver Price

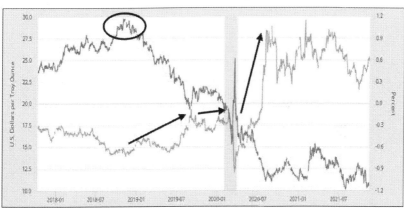

Source: Federal Reserve Bank of St. Louis

Silver clearly enjoys nearly the same inverse relationship with real rates as does gold.

We are in an environment where the Federal Reserve is generally keeping interest rates artificially low and has repeatedly stated that it wants higher inflation. In fact, it's willing to let inflation run well above its 2% target for some time in order compensate for low (below 2%) rates that persisted between 2015 and 2020. This is called "average-inflation targeting." And it's going to lead to a lot more inflation, persistently low real rates, and much higher silver prices.

As it turns out, the Fed is getting the inflation it secretly wants.

The following chart shows the "Real Yield" you can earn on a 10-year U.S. Treasury bond.

"Real Yield" on 10-Year U.S. Treasury

Source: stansberryresearch.com

After accounting for inflation this bond is losing about 5% of its purchasing power every year. That's the worst in 50 years.

As a result, we have the perfect environment for silver to perform exceedingly well.

Key Takeaways

- Real rates are the key to predicting future silver prices.

- They are simple to understand: Real rate = current interest rate minus the inflation rate.

- Silver performs well when real rates are falling and/or negative.

Chapter 16: What Things Really Cost

Because silver acts as a hedge against inflation, it's important to know just what the rate of inflation is at any given point in time.

The CPI is the Consumer Price Index, and the CPI-U is the index reflecting urban consumers.

The CPI measures the average change in prices over time for a basket of goods and services. This is also commonly called the inflation level. The U.S. Bureau of Labor Statistics (BLS) has reported the CPI since 1913.

And while we're talking about inflation, keep in mind that the statistics the BLS provides have changed and are "adjusted" to account for economic value and technological improvements.

In other words, central planners want us to believe that our cost of living is only increasing *slowly*.

But the real story is much different.

This next chart shows what happened to inflation during and after the COVID-19 pandemic. There was a short-lived fall in prices in the first few months, then prices quickly resumed their previous levels.

But one year later, as all the government stimulus kicked in and the world economy slowly opened back up, huge pent-up demand and supply chain disruptions began quickly pushing prices higher.

Consumer Price Index, All Urban Consumers: Less Food & Energy U.S. City Average

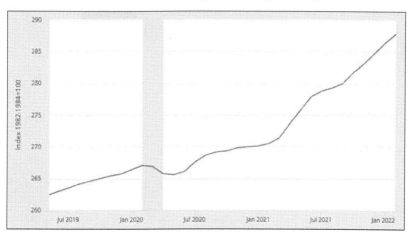

Source: Federal Reserve Bank of St. Louis

Just 18 months after the pandemic hit, U.S. inflation had rocketed to levels not seen in 40 years.

The Federal Reserve was finally getting the higher inflation it had been wanting so badly.

By March 2022, U.S. inflation had soared to 8.5% over the previous 12 months - a 41-year high. If you consider you'd need to be about 10 years old to remember an inflationary environment, then anyone under 50 today doesn't understand what it's really like. So, two thirds of the U.S. population have not truly experienced sustained high inflation.

And real inflation usually runs much, much higher than official statistics. Remember, silver moves based on real rates: interest minus inflation. More importantly, silver rallies on low and/or falling real rates.

If the Federal Reserve holds rates down or even raises them slowly as inflation races higher, real rates can fall even faster - creating an-almost-perfect environment for silver prices to soar.

John Williams of shadowstats.com - which crunches the numbers to provide "real" alternatives to government inflation statistics - tells us that "in general terms, methodological shifts in government reporting have depressed reported inflation, moving the concept of the CPI away from being a measure of the cost of living needed to maintain a constant standard of living."

So, ShadowStats provides its own alternate CPI based on the calculation methods used in 1980. And the difference between the current CPI-U and ShadowStats' numbers is shocking.

And I mean....*shocking.*

Consumer Inflation –
Official vs. ShadowStats (1980-Based) Alternate

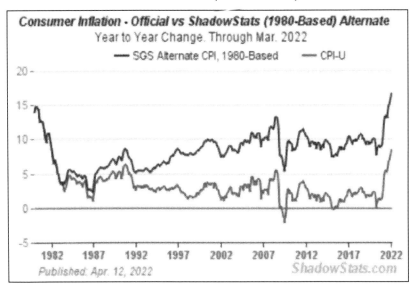

Source: shadowstats.com

Have you ever wondered why the prices you see, and the cost-of-living increases you experience, often don't match "official inflation" levels?

Well, now you know why.

As the above chart demonstrates, there's been roughly an 8% difference between the ShadowStats consumer inflation and official CPI-U inflation in recent decades.

And because ShadowStats bases its calculations on a 1980-baseline, you're talking about a divergence that's existed for decades.

That's right...decades.

And this isn't an accident.

We're talking about deliberate Washington subterfuge.

Workers demanding pay raises when Washington or other governmental bureaucracies tell us that inflation is surging.

By contrast, low inflation leaves us feeling complacent - even content - which dampens those pesky raise demands.

But workers are still the losers: The goods and services we consume, along with the taxes on them, continue to rise. And that's why, although paychecks have grown over the last 40 years, they don't buy more than they used to.

Consider how detrimental inflation can be on a currency - and how much it hits us right in the wallet.

The following chart shows that your $100 today will be worth just $59 in 10 years with inflation running at just 5.4% annually. At higher inflation rates, your purchasing power falls even faster.

Fall in Value of $100 over 10 years at 5.4% Annual Inflation

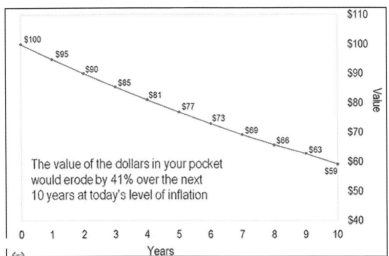

Source: *Palm Beach Research Group, U.S. Bureau of Labor*

Looking back at the ShadowStats chart, you now fully understand that you're losing purchasing power at an accelerating rate.

And as we see in the graphic that follows, our paychecks just aren't growing fast enough to keep pace with the real growth in the cost of living. Purchasing power has been nearly flat for more than 40 years.

Average Hourly Wages in the U.S. vs. Purchasing Power

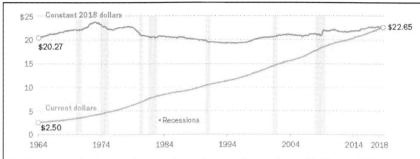

Note: Data for wages of production and non-supervisory employees on private non-farm payrolls. "Constant 2018 dollars" describes wages adjusted for inflation. "Current dollars" describes wages reported in the value of the currency when received. "Purchasing power" refers to the amount of goods or services that can be bought per unit of currency.
Source: U.S. Bureau of Labor Statistics.

Source: Pew Research

The future isn't any better - in fact, it's downright bleak; I can almost guarantee that this shortfall is only going to get worse. While wages could increase as inflation does, I don't see that happening. Inflation is likely to race ahead of any wage gains. It may feel like people are earning more and getting richer, but that's a mirage: The reality is that our true cost of living will rise faster. That will cause most folks to become poorer, not richer, without even understanding why.

This is what happened in the late 1960s and the 1970s. That's where we're headed again. And it's why we're having this long conversation about silver.

Let me offer some additional proof.

The growth of money in circulation was significant in the 1970s and clearly led to inflation.

There are several different measures of the total money supply in the economy. Some incorporate more components, while others include less. The M2 money supply measure includes cash, checking deposits, savings deposits, money market securities, mutual funds, and other time deposits.

This chart plots the growth of the M2 money supply against the inflation rate.

Inflation Rate and M2 Money Supply/capita
Year-over-year %, 1900-2020

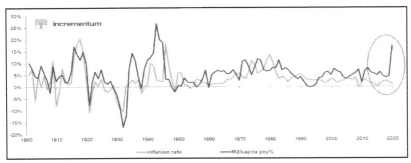

Source: Incrementum AG

It's clear that, in periods when the M2 money supply rises, the inflation rate is never far behind. This happened in the 1930s and 1940s and again in the 1970s.

And silver soared during each of those stretches.

Over the last couple of years, massive amounts of stimulus have caused exponential growth in the money supply. Inflation is now following closely behind. And this sets the stage for much higher silver prices.

Key Takeaways

- The official Consumer Price Index (CPI) is rising rapidly, though it's vastly understated.
- According to ShadowStats research, inflation is likely <u>higher</u> than official rates by 8% annually.
- Cash is quickly being devalued, dramatically cutting our buying power.
- Money supply has exploded higher. Inflation has always followed, leading to higher silver.

Chapter 17: Money Velocity and Hoarding

One important factor in kick-starting inflation is money velocity.

Over time, that means the rate at which a dollar changes hands in the economy, from one entity or person to another.

The next chart demonstrates money velocity has been falling dramatically since the late 1990s. Interestingly, this coincides with the big ramp-up in public debt since then.

Remember, the more money in the system, the more transactions it takes to maintain the same velocity. And money velocity absolutely crashed when the pandemic lockdowns were followed by massive stimulus money printing and debt expansion.

M2 Money Velocity, Q1/1900 - Q1/2021

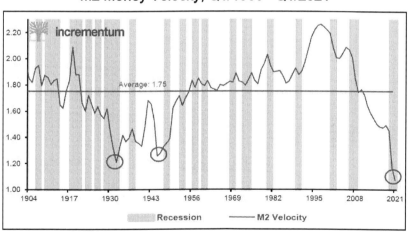

Source: Incrementum AG

But as COVID-19 pandemic restrictions on business and leisure fade, money velocity will kick into high gear. The trigger is likely to be a releasing of pent-up demand. As the economy "reopens," people are eager to travel, renovate, go to concerts and sporting events, or just enjoy a restaurant meal.

There is precedent in 1933, at the depths of the Great Depression, and in 1946, after World War II. Note these lows in the chart above. Both times dramatic steps were taken by central planners to trigger inflation.

In the 2021 edition of *In Gold We Trust* - the yearly review on gold investing published by asset manager Incrementum AG - authors Ronald-Peter Stoeferle and Mark J. Valek stated:

> *In 1933 and 1946, the velocity of money was similarly low, and in both cases the US government resorted to radical measures. In January 1934, it devalued the US dollar against gold by almost 70%, and in the period 1946- 1951 it enforced financial repression in cooperation with the Federal Reserve, which capped interest rates at a low level. Both times, this massive intervention resulted in significantly higher inflation rates in the years that followed. Currently, the velocity of money is at even lower levels than in 1933 or 1946. We expect history to repeat itself and central banks to seek their salvation in financial repression.*

Taking global debt to historical record highs while holding rates down at 5,000-year lows is stoking inflation like we haven't seen in a long time.

And there's one more aspect you should consider about inflation and money velocity: **inflationary psychology, also known as hoarding.**

That's the phenomenon whereby consumers come to accept that inflation is finally entrenched, and prices will continue to rise strongly for the foreseeable future.

As a result, they try to "get ahead" of inflation. They start to spend more quickly and buy in larger quantities than they normally would. They figure they can save money by buying sooner rather than later, when prices are expected to be higher. This is not limited to consumers, but also businesses and institutions who may also speed up their buying.

This can even become a self-fulfilling prophecy - a feedback loop.

As consumers spend more and forego saving, this "hoarding mentality" can accelerate money velocity in the economy: the rate at which dollar changes hands. This tends to speed up inflation even faster, further reinforcing the inflationary psychology mindset.

Ultimately, it can lead to much, much higher inflation, and even asset bubbles.

We may not be there yet. But real estate prices that soared almost immediately after the COVID-19 pandemic hit, and then kept rising right through the ongoing pandemic and beyond, look like a telltale sign of inflationary psychology.

And this is just one sector of the economy. Small-ticket items like consumer goods and other non-perishables are much easier to "front run" before prices increase further.

Naturally, hard assets like silver, along with silver stocks, will be strong beneficiaries when inflationary psychology takes hold.

Key Takeaways

- Money Velocity is the rate at which currency changes hands in the economy.

- The more money in the system, the more transactions are needed to maintain velocity.

- Central planners devalue currencies and hold interest rates low to trigger inflation, but inflationary psychology can dramatically accelerate money velocity.

Chapter 18: Silver, Gold, and Commodities Sensing Inflation

Precious metals have been sensing this. It's why they've risen so substantially, with the global money supply up fivefold in the last 20 years.

Silver and gold have kicked into high gear since late 2019. Silver prices doubled from mid-2019 to mid-2021. But that's just the opening act.

Sustained high inflation, coupled with low interest rates, creates an environment of extended negative real interest rates. That's when silver and gold thrive.

With money so cheap - what low interest rates really mean - record global debt will keep expanding as governments continue to borrow and spend. That coupled with a resurgence of money velocity means inflation rears its ugly head.

In the 1970s, the US money supply multiplied, causing the dollar to *lose two-thirds of its purchasing power over that decade alone.*

This chart of the Producer Price Index for all commodities shows what happened to commodity prices during the 1970s. These are the raw commodities manufacturers buy to produce things.

Producer Price Index, All Commodities, 1970 - 1982

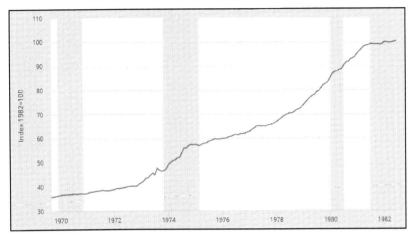

Source: Federal Reserve Bank of St. Louis

The index rose from 36 to 93, causing prices to soar over 250%. That matches the rate of inflation and the dollar's loss of purchasing power, as these manufacturer costs are passed on to consumers.

Research from Crescat Capital shows that, between 1965 and 1980, there were three distinct waves of inflation, suggesting that these hefty price spikes don't usually come in a gradual and orderly fashion. In fact, the following chart suggests that it tends to happen in a pattern of rising waves.

The Three Inflationary Waves of the 1970s

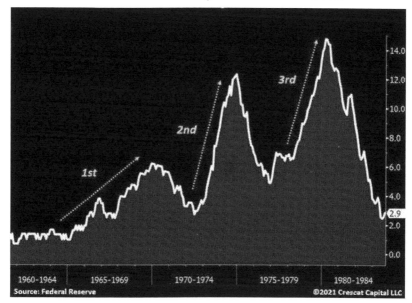

Source: Crescat Capital, Federal Reserve

As the U.S. Federal Reserve and government tried to alternate between fighting inflation and supporting economic growth, the boom-and-bust cycle wreaked havoc on the economy.

What's different about that period is debt-to-GDP levels were close to 35% - where today they're closer to 130%. With such massive debt at the government, corporate and personal levels, central banks find it nearly impossible to raise rates without crushing the economy.

Interestingly, the ratio of commodities to equities tends to follow inflation quite closely over decades. As we can see from the following chart, when commodities gain over stocks, as they did during the 1970s, this ratio clearly tracks inflation.

And now with inflation surging higher, a similar rise in the commodities to equities ratio should follow.

Commodities to Equities Ratio vs. Inflation 1970 - 2021

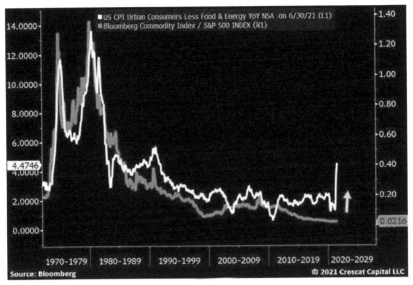

Source: Crescat Capital, Bloomberg

This next chart shows what happened to stocks, gold, and silver in the 1970s.

Most people would be shocked to know that *the Dow Jones and S&P 500 were basically flat for a dismal decade **before** accounting for inflation*. The lines at the bottom of the chart are the overlapping Dow Jones and S&P 500.

Meanwhile, gold generated a 1,400% return, yet silver was the clear leader with a 3,700% return.

S&P 500 vs. Dow Jones vs. Gold vs. Silver 1970s

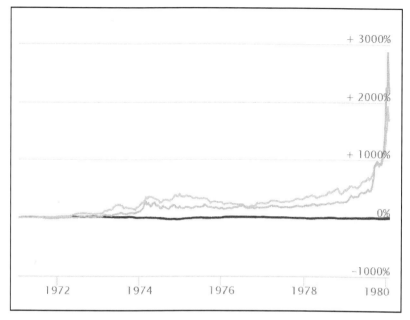

Source: longtermtrends.net

Now let's look at this same chart from 2000 until early 2022.

There are a few big standouts.

First, most investors probably think stocks have been the place to be since 2000, but that's plain wrong. Gold is up an impressive 575%, while silver has produced a healthy 385% gain - *both metals easily beating stocks which gained about 200%.*

The second takeaway is that despite silver's strong performance, gold is still ahead, for now. I say for now because, as you'll seen in Chapter 28, silver has always outperformed gold in bull markets. And I expect silver to do the same in this current precious-metals bull market. On the other hand, stocks are likely due for a period of subpar returns once again.

S&P 500 vs. Dow Jones vs. Gold vs. Silver
Dec. 1999 - Mar. 2022

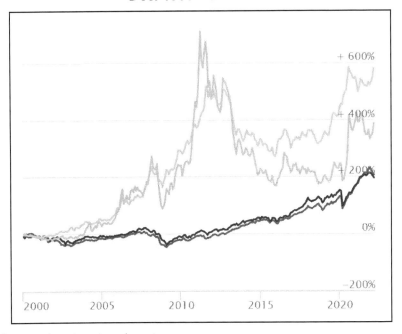

Source: longtermtrends.net

Now let's look at a list of major commodities and their performance over one year to April 2021. Prices for nearly all resources have soared, many up 50% and several up more than 250%.

One-year Commodity Returns
May 2020 - April 2021

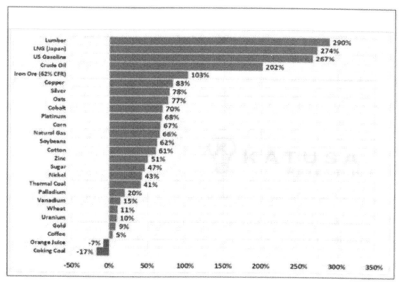

Source: Katusa Research

Thanks to unprecedented money-printing to stimulate the economy and kick-start post-pandemic inflation, we've entered the early stages of a new secular commodities boom.

And with financial repression maintaining low interest rates, prices for nearly everything are soaring, and they will continue doing so for years. Meanwhile, savers are punished with ultralow interest rates.

Key Takeaways

- When inflation rises, commodities and precious metals outperform stocks.
- Silver and gold easily beat stocks in the 1970s, and again since 2000.
- Commodity prices soared post-pandemic with ongoing financial repression.

In **Part II**, I took you behind the scenes for a glimpse at the kinds of strategies central planners use to manipulate interest rates, money supply, and inflation.

By expanding the money supply and holding rates low, they try to stimulate the economy and kick-start inflation. They use tactics, like financial repression and negative interest rates, which wouldn't even exist if money were allowed to trade as a free market.

When the COVID-19 pandemic hit I saw how governments were reacting. I understood they were using "helicopter money" (Modern Monetary Theory) and other easy-money policies to support and stimulate the economy. That's when I realized that we were entering a new era of much higher inflation, and an acceleration phase for silver.

The secret key of negative real rates is our best indicator. It tells us when we're in an environment that leads to rapidly rising silver prices. Consumer price inflation, money supply and money velocity are also good predictors of where silver prices are headed.

Commodities are very sensitive to inflation. When they consistently outperform stocks, commodities tend to track inflation higher. This has clearly started to happen. That's why silver and gold handily beat stocks in the 1970s, and again since 2000.

It's time for you to fight back.

Silver - and silver-related investments - are amongst the best ways to do that and win. As you'll see in **Part III**, silver is uniquely positioned to thrive in this kind of environment.

I'll show you how silver has some of the same inflation and safe-haven characteristics as gold. But you'll also learn how, unlike gold, silver is used in so many ways, it's indispensable in our everyday lives.

And that makes it an unmatched investment for profits going forward.

Part III: Silver – The Irreplaceable Metal

Introduction:
There's Nothing Quite Like Silver

Silver has proven itself as money over millennia. But it also has so many practical applications that, in many ways, it just can't be replaced.

Unlike any other, silver has dual roles as a monetary and industrial metal. And as we move through the next several years, that will set it clearly apart from other commodities.

Silver really is a world unto itself, with distinct supply and demand characteristics, macro forces, and dedicated investors.

Although silver has many features like gold, it's much cheaper. And some of its physical properties are actually superior.

In the periodic table of elements, silver is No. 47, and its symbol is Ag. That's from the Latin word Argentum, which itself originates from the Greek word for "shiny."

In **Part III**, we're going to look at differences between the gold and silver markets. We'll examine where silver comes from and constraints on its supply.

Then we'll see the varied uses of silver, from industrial applications to medical, jewelry and investment demand. We'll even look at some emerging applications that could lead to vast new sources of demand many have never even considered.

Chapter 19: Gold is Gold

It's estimated that about 200,000 metric tons of gold have been extracted from the earth throughout history.

Gold mined since 1950 accounts for about two-thirds of that total.

But, with most gold used as some form of investment, *the bulk of it is still around in the form of bars, coins, or jewelry.*

It's true that gold, like silver, is also money and used in industry. But its role as a store of value is much more pronounced than any other application.

Gold jewelry can be seen as a form of investment because it retains its value over time. It's very popular in China and India to buy gold as a method of savings, especially because it can always be sold for cash if needed.

If we add up investment, jewelry, and central bank holdings, these three categories account for 92% of gold demand. That leaves just 8% of gold finding its way into applications such as electronics (LED, 5G infrastructure and devices, memory chips, printed circuit boards), industry and dentistry.

Distribution of Gold Demand Worldwide by Sector in 2020

Source: Statista

So, most of the gold demand is for investment, with less than 10% being consumed.

The annual supply of gold, around 120 million ounces, is worth about $230 billion. In contrast, the annual silver supply is around 1 billion ounces, for a total value of about $25 billion. *On this basis, the gold market is roughly ten times larger than the silver market.*

In the 1970s, governments held large inventories of silver because they still used it in their coinage. By the early 1980s, they still held about 330 million ounces.

Then they began to sell off their stockpiles. Today just the United States, Mexico and India still hold about 45 million ounces in total. On the other hand, central banks currently hold more than 35,000 tonnes of gold, and they've been aggressive net buyers since 2009.

World Official Central Bank Gold Holdings 2000 - 2020

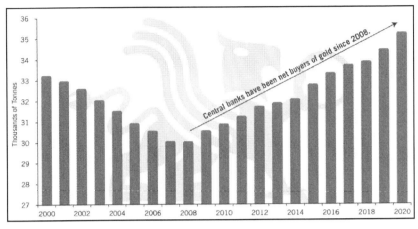

Source: BMG Group Inc.

But with silver being a much smaller market, it's easy to see that consistent, elevated buying could push prices dramatically higher over a relatively short time.

Key Takeaways

- About 90% of gold is purchased to hold as a form of investment.

- Governments used to stockpile silver, mostly for coinage, but no longer.

- Central banks have been big net buyers of gold since 2009.

Chapter 20: Have We Reached "Peak Silver"?

It's estimated, according to The Royal Mint, that silver can be found in the earth's crust at a rate of about 75 parts per billion. So, there are likely still 7.5 trillion kilograms of silver sprinkled around.

Naturally, that silver is more concentrated in some places than in others, which is what makes silver mining possible.

About 1.4 billion kilograms or 45.5 billion ounces of silver have been extracted from the earth throughout human history.

The United States Geological Survey (USGS) estimates there were roughly 10 billion ounces of above-ground silver available back in 1950. Fast forward 30 years to 1980, and that fell by two-thirds to just 3.5 billion ounces.

The Silver Institute estimates the total has since fallen in half, with identifiable silver bullion inventories sitting around 1.7 billion ounces. Most of the drop is because silver is no longer part of coinage, so just a handful of governments and central banks hold insignificant amounts.

Contrast that with gold.

About 200,000 tonnes or just over 6 billion ounces of gold have been mined to date. But with industry consuming very little gold, most of what's been extracted throughout history is still with us today.

Approximately half is in jewelry, about 20% is held as investment, and governments and their central banks own some 17%. As a result, there are about 2.5 billion ounces of gold bullion inventories between private investment and official holdings.

In other words, there's roughly 50% more gold bullion available today than there is silver. The world has been consuming more silver than it's been mining for years. What's more, Metals Focus and the Silver Institute forecast supply deficits to deepen and persist for the next several years.

Silver Supply Deficit Forecast to Grow and Persist

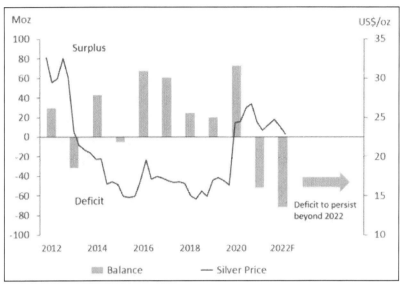

Source: Metals Focus, The Silver Institute

Deepening silver supply deficits, combined with demand, has set the stage for a perfect storm of rising silver prices.

Now let's take a close look at where silver comes from and the implications for the future of silver markets.

Key Takeaways

- Silver inventories have been falling for decades.
- There is about 50% more gold bullion inventory than silver available today.

- Silver is forecast to suffer worsening deficits over the next decade.

Chapter 21: Silver's Quirky Supply Profile

Silver's not only exceptional because it's prized as money and it's irreplaceable in industry. It's also unique for how it's typically found in nature.

According to the Silver Institute, about 80% of annual silver supply is from mine production, with most of the 20% balance coming from recycling.

It's also important to understand some of the intricacies of silver mine supply. A primary silver mine is one where silver is the main commodity produced. Contrary to what you might think, those mines are rare.

Mined Silver by Co-Metals Production

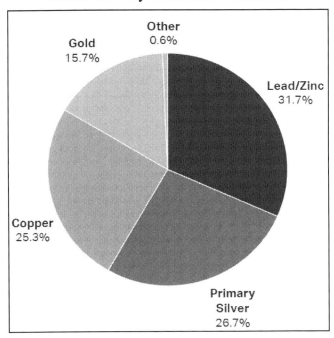

Source: Metals Focus, ICSG, ILZSG

Few realize that only 26.7% of mined silver in 2020 was from primary silver mines. That leaves fully 73.3% of silver extracted as a by-product of mining *other* metals. Lead/zinc mines produce 31.7% of mined silver, copper mines contribute 25.3%, and gold mines account for 15.7%.

With just over one quarter of mined silver coming from primary silver mines, there are huge implications for the supply side of the silver market.

Miners of lead, zinc, copper, and gold, who also produce some silver, tend to view it as a minor source of revenue. Some miners sell part of or all their silver output to a streaming/royalty company in return for a large advance, or cash payments at a big discount to spot prices.

The proceeds might help finance the development and/or construction of a mine, or they may supplement the income from producing their primary metals. When silver is "sold off" as a stream or royalty, there is less incentive to produce more.

Consider the following example.

Let's say demand rises substantially, causing the silver price to jump by 20%. For most products the manufacturer would simply "crank up production" to respond to higher demand and capture the additional profits.

But mining is a challenging business. Expanding an existing mine means permitting, financing, and adding to processing capacity. A new mine means dealing with long lead times to find economic silver deposits, financing, permitting, and ultimately building *before* producing.

Even just restarting an old mine with a proven deposit can require financing, engineering studies, dewatering, underground tunnel, or shaft remediation and permitting before bringing it back online. Sometimes, there are considerable social, environmental, and/or geopolitical hurdles that are very costly, time-consuming, or even impossible to overcome.

Then layer on top the fact that nearly three-quarters of silver comes from mining other metals.

So, miners of gold, lead, zinc, and copper, who also happen to produce silver, can't just open the spigot to get more just because its price has risen. Many times, miners will simply accept the higher price for the silver they already produce and not respond otherwise. They just see the silver revenues as helpful to offset costs for their primary metals. Or, with higher silver prices, they start processing the same quantity of ore, but at lower grade with less silver content. That means they could make the same or more profits, while silver output *declines*.

This makes silver production inelastic to the silver price. That means silver production will often not respond to, or may even fall, with a rise in the silver price.

And that can fuel *even higher silver prices*. Because one of the few things that would spur higher silver production is not just higher prices but *sustained* higher prices. Silver miners will need to see silver prices rise and stay high, likely for years, before even thinking about trying to produce more.

Keep in mind that silver and gold are among the few investments whose rising price tends to beget more buying.

Rather than being contrarians, many less experienced investors "panic-buy" as they see prices climb and are fearful of missing out. They worry that if they wait any longer, they'll just have to pay more. That fear factor can be a very powerful motivator, as we'll see in Chapter 31.

Key Takeaways

- Only 27% of mined silver comes from primary silver mines.

- Miners of silver by-product are less motivated to produce more even with higher prices.

- Silver supply is inelastic; supply doesn't automatically increase with rising prices.

Chapter 22: A Brief History of Silver Mining

Historians tell us that silver mining dates back as far as 6,000 years ago.

It's one of the first five metals to be discovered. Silver objects dating to 4000 BC have been found by archaeologists.

The Silver Institute says the earliest known silver mines were in Anatolia (modern-day Turkey) around 3000 BC. Silver as money was likely instrumental in helping early civilizations of the Near East and Ancient Greece to thrive.

Some 1,800 years later, around 1200 BC, it seems Greece became the center of silver mining. The Laurium mines supplied the area, with silver eventually becoming ancient Athens' currency. Around 100 BC, Spain evolved as the global center of silver mining, supplying the Roman Empire with currency to use along Asian spice routes.

Centuries later, Columbus's discovery of the New World in 1492 became the single most pivotal event in silver mining history.

That's because Spain's conquest of the Americas dramatically increased silver production, especially from Mexico, Bolivia, and Peru. Between 1500 and 1800, silver production from these three nations alone represented fully 85% of global output. Spain had hit the proverbial jackpot.

As Niall Ferguson details in his book *The Ascent of Money*, Peru's Cerro Rico - the "rich hill," was seen as a mountain of pure silver in Potosí. Unfortunately for the Incas, who were ultimately forced to work the mines, Spanish thirst for silver was unquenchable.

Conditions were extremely harsh, with mortality running high from accidents and a polluted mining environment. A dwindling supply of natives caused the Spaniards to import thousands of African slaves to replace them. It was hideous and reprehensible.

But for the Spanish conquerors, the ends justified the means. From the mid-1500s to the late 1700s, Cerro Rico generated 45,000 tons of pure silver. That's the equivalent of over 1.4 billion ounces. In the first few decades, this new supply of silver was dramatic. Although it was meant to help pay for Spain's wars of conquest, there was so much new coinage that it triggered strong inflation.

This rapid boost to the money supply affected all of Europe, with a "price inflation" that lasted from the 1540s to the 1640s. After three centuries without sustained higher prices, food costs rose decidedly. The cost of living was up seven times during that period. Although that looks tame by today's standards, working out to about 2% annually, it was radical at the time.

Today, the risk of a sudden flood of new silver supply is extremely remote. That's true for all the reasons I've detailed so far. Demand is high and growing. Supply is tight and shrinking. And, until now, technology doesn't allow us to produce vast amounts of silver over a very short period.

Maybe a massive, super high-grade deposit will be found that floods silver supply and depresses prices. But given how long we've extracted silver from the earth, I wouldn't bet on that happening soon. In all likeliness, nearly all the Cerro Ricos have already been found and mined out.

Instead, the real threat is from the fiat money supply. As I mentioned earlier, nearly one-quarter of all U.S. dollars in existence were created between January 2020 and June 2021. Because it has no intrinsic value and is mostly in the form of digits, a greater concern is governments accelerating the growth

120

of fiat money.

Ferguson also points out in *The Ascent of Money* that "Money is worth only what someone else is willing to give you for it. An increase in its supply will not make society richer, though it may enrich the government that monopolizes the production of money. Other things being equal, monetary expansion will merely make prices higher."

Now that we've looked very briefly at silver mining through history, let's look at where the metal is mined today. And with that, we'll explore some of the key challenges of mining silver.

Key Takeaways

- The first known silver mines trace back 5,000 years to modern-day Turkey.
- Columbus' discovery of the Americas brought massive new silver supplies to Europe.
- That caused the first inflation in centuries, lasting 100 years.

Chapter 23: Where Silver Actually Comes From

As with so many things, the first silver mine was in the old world.

But with the discovery of the Americas, Europeans hit the silver jackpot.

Today, nearly half of mined silver comes from Latin America.

Mexico is by far the largest supplier, producing 196.7 million ounces in 2021. China is next, with 112.9 million ounces of production, followed closely by Peru, whose output was 107.9 million ounces. The next group contributes less than 50 million ounces annually, with Chile, Australia, Russia, Poland, the U.S., Bolivia, and Argentina producing between 26.5 million and 43 million ounces each.

What's striking about the silver supply from mining is how rapidly it's been falling. In 2016 global mine supply peaked then began dropping for the next four straight years. A small supply bounce is expected, but that's likely to peak in 2024 before falling once again. And that peak is not expected to surpass the 2016 high.

Mine Supply by Country, 1990-2025E by Million Ounces

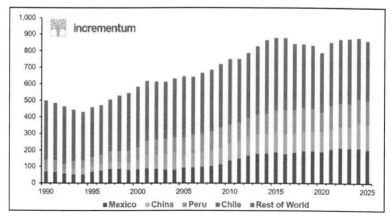

Source: The Silver Institute, Incrementum AG

In short, I think we may have reached "peak silver" mine supply.

After all, mine production topped out just shy of 900 million ounces at 899.4 million in 2016, according to the Silver Institute. By 2020, it had dropped by 12.8% to 784.4 million ounces. In 2020, silver mines produced 6% less than in 2019 - but to be fair, a good portion of that decrease was related to COVID-19 pandemic restrictions.

Jurisdiction Matters

With half of the silver mine supply coming from three countries - Mexico, Peru, and China - geopolitical concerns are real. Silver's importance to high-tech industries, including electric/hybrid vehicles, solar power, medicine, 5G telecommunications and mobile technologies, should give us pause.

China is a leading manufacturer in many of these sectors and may not hesitate to limit silver exports. There is precedent.

Controlling 97% of production, China nearly completely dominates the global supply of rare earths, 17 elements with magnetic and conductive properties. These are crucial in the production of everything from high-tech military equipment to more common smartphones.

In 2010 the Chinese government, which already had export duties and quotas, reduced quotas by 40%, saying these were necessary for "environmental protection." This caused rare earth prices to explode higher, with opponents heavily criticizing the move as protectionist. Of course, domestic manufacturers had a major advantage, as these same rare earth materials sold at much lower prices within China.

The U.S. challenged China's position by bringing a case against it to the World Trade Organization (WTO). Supported by the European Union and Japan, the U.S. argued the quotas were against the WTO's rules when China signed on in 2001. China lost, appealed, then ultimately lost its appeal. Of course, by then, it was already 2015, and China finally removed its export quotas. But the rest of the world had to accept higher prices in the meantime.

In early 2021, Chinese export restrictions on rare earth minerals were back on the table in the wake of deteriorating China-U.S. relations. The Chinese were considering sanctions against U.S. military contractors Lockheed Martin, Boeing, and Raytheon since they were selling arms to Taiwan. China continues to claim Taiwan as part of its territory, though Taiwan is a self-ruling island.

As much as they may need each other, China and the West often go through antagonistic periods, arguing over unfair trade practices, intellectual property, and even human rights as common themes. The point is, as silver grows in importance, China may choose to limit its exports to the West.

Research published by World Developments examined whether mining companies are compensated for geopolitical risk. In other words, they wanted to know if miners in higher-risk jurisdictions get more favourable terms.

As it turns out, the answer is no, though the reasons are difficult to pinpoint. It's thought that governments in developing countries demand higher compensation from miners since their general tax revenues are relatively low. They may be seeking higher tax revenues, especially from foreign firms, to help support the existing political system. As well, higher taxes are demanded to provide social, economic, and environmental support to local communities.

Remember, a valuable deposit can't be moved. That makes it an easy target for a government willing to change the rules and extract a higher take from the mining company.

The supply of various minerals is often at risk of geopolitical tensions and internal politics. Peru is a prime example. The country is the world's No. 2 silver and copper supplier. Remember, over 25% of the annual silver mine supply is a by-product of copper production.

Despite the dire need for more of both metals, Peru may face headwinds to major new investments for some time. Pedro Castillo was elected President in July 2021. During his campaign, the former schoolteacher first threatened to nationalize mines, then softened his approach by suggesting a major tax revision.

Castillo proposed a new tax of up to 70% on mining profits and royalties on mineral sales. And this, despite mining accounting for almost 60% of the country's exports. Once elected, he softened his tone once again but still proposed to review contracts with mining companies to hike their taxes.

Though less impactful to the silver supply, even Chile's 47 million ounces of annual production could face challenges. Keep in mind this nation contributes more than a quarter of global copper production: 60% of Chile's exports, and 15% of gross domestic product.

And rising copper prices have leaders hungry to tax profits even more. Higher taxes up to 75% on profits from copper above $4/lb. are popular, with nearly three-quarters of Chileans being supportive. There's no doubt that dramatically higher taxes would stifle future investments by mining companies, leading to falling output.

At a time when national fiscal deficits and debts are ballooning, exacerbated by the COVID-19 pandemic, desperate leaders are quick to take aim at mining companies. Rising revenues, thanks to rising metals prices, make for easy targets.

What those leaders, as well as their voters, forget is that higher taxes on mining companies ultimately mean even higher metals prices. And that will manifest itself as a higher cost of living. There is no escape. But investors can flip the situation to their advantage, investing in those metals and their miners for rising profits.

These risks demonstrate how fragile silver mine production is. In fact, given such rising geopolitical challenges, just maintaining current silver production levels may be difficult. And all of this is unfolding with a backdrop of steadily rising demand from industry and investment alike.

Key Takeaways

- Nearly half of mined silver comes from Latin America.
- Silver mine supply may have peaked in recent years.
- Some governments increase mining taxes to boost income and support local communities.

Chapter 24: The Best Places to Mine Silver Today

In 1857, prospectors and settlors rushed to Nevada in the hopes of getting rich from a new silver discovery.

Over the next decade, half a billion dollars of silver was mined from the Comstock Lode. It became America's biggest silver rush.

The Grosh brothers, veterans of the California Gold Rush, had found traces of gold on the eastern slope of Mount Davidson. But their prize was a massive silver vein: a very high purity bluish clay. Sadly, the Grosh brothers died the next year, one from infection and the other from hypothermia in a snowstorm – hazards of prospecting in the 1800s. Their friend, Henry Comstock, lacked funding and couldn't capitalize on the discovery. So, he and others sold their shares on the cheap. But Comstock's name stuck to the discovery.

The moral of the story: finding the proverbial "motherlode" of silver is one thing; but getting that silver out of the ground safely and profitably is another.

Geopolitical risks make jurisdiction a crucial factor in choosing silver investments.

Think of it like this. A big, valuable silver deposit can't be moved. So, its owner is at the mercy of the government. If that government is friendly and follows the rule of law, risk is lower. If the government is corrupt, changes often, and caters to special interest groups, it could nationalize the mine or impose heavy taxes. Risk is higher.

In my view, that currently makes Canada, the United States, Mexico, Australia, and some parts of Europe and South America the more attractive options. Let's look at the first three more closely.

With its 196.7 million ounces of annual silver production, Mexico is the clear leader among silver-producing nations, accounting for nearly 23% of global silver output. Understanding its mineral endowment and storied silver mining history lets us appreciate just how significant this one country is to the silver market.

Mexico is attractive for many reasons. First, that's where the silver is, and Mexico has been producing the metal in quantity for more than 500 years. From the 1570s to the 1630s, Peru was the silver leader. But, by the 1700s, Mexico leapfrogged it, with silver representing more than 70% of that new leader's exports through the 1870s.

The largest-producing state is centrally located Zacatecas, which generates about 2,100 metric tons annually. Next is Chihuahua State with 1,200 metric tons, followed by Durango with 819 metric tons, and Sonora with 632. These make up the bulk of Mexican production.

Geologically, Mexico is attractive. Its terrain is one of the most tectonically active and complex, having created the Sierra Madre Mountain chains. Much of the silver found today is linked to the Sierra Madre Occidental range.

Mexican laws give preference to mineral exploration and extraction over any other land use, allowing for 100% private ownership, including foreign ownership. And with mining having such a long and established history, it's a place that is mostly welcoming to the industry.

Mining represents 8.3% of industrial GDP and 2.5% of national GDP. While concessions are required to explore and extract silver, they must be negotiated with surface landowners to access the land. Because it's a member of the North American Free Trade Agreement (NAFTA), in addition to having agreements with several other major economies, Mexico's environmental laws have become increasingly strict. Mining runs deep in this developing nation, and I expect it will continue to be a silver powerhouse for decades to come.

Its neighbor to the north - the United States - has two states that stand out today for silver mining: Nevada and Idaho.

Nevada is a top jurisdiction for gold production today, yet it's known as the "Silver State." The Comstock Lode discovery made Nevada the first important silver mining district in the U.S., which eventually led to several more silver discoveries in the state. Comstock went on to produce an impressive 192 million silver ounces, and the Tonopah silver district produced over 174 million silver ounces.

Alaska produces more silver than Nevada, much of it as a byproduct of mining other metals. Based on investment attractiveness, the Fraser Institute ranked Nevada as the world's top mining jurisdiction in 2020. If it were a country, Nevada would be the world's fifth-largest gold producer.

But some of Nevada's past silver-producing areas have made it one of the highest-grade silver districts in the world. Nevada's silver potential has been rediscovered in recent years, and it's been getting a lot more attention. There have been numerous exploration efforts in districts that historically produced huge quantities of silver. The idea that "the best place to look for a mine is next to an old one" continues to ring true. But interestingly several brand-new, sizeable discoveries have been made in areas that were not previously known for silver or even other mining activity.

Despite so much focus on Nevada's obvious gold endowment, it seems inevitable that silver will get a lot more attention. And with the state's excellent infrastructure, pro-mining regime and ease of access, I expect Nevada to become somewhat of a silver powerhouse as well.

Idaho is the United States' undisputed historic silver capital. Gold was first discovered in 1863, but in the late 1870s miners realized silver was the prize as they unearthed lots of it in high concentration.

Northern Idaho's small panhandle area is called the "Silver Valley." Many of the mines run very deep, producing down to 5,000 feet or more. One mine alone, the Sunshine Mine, produced over 360 million ounces of silver.

Historically known as the Coeur d'Alene district, the Silver Valley has produced more than 1.2 billion ounces of silver in the last 140 years. It's the U.S.'s largest silver district and one of the world's three largest, while still being successfully and profitably mined today. The other top two districts are Pachuca-Real del Monte in Mexico, and Potosi in Bolivia, both of which have generated over 1 billion silver ounces.

In Canada, two areas stand out for silver mining: The Yukon Territory and Northern British Columbia. The Yukon has a long and storied history with mining, though it's best known for its gold rush. Gold was first discovered by a local miner in 1896, and by 1899 some 100,000 prospectors made their way to the Klondike region of the Yukon. Most left empty-handed. But successful mining in the Yukon would soon get another lift.

Government records indicate that, between 1913 and 1989, the Keno Hill Mining District of the Yukon produced over 200 million ounces of silver from just 5.3 million tons of ore. Grades averaged 44 ounces of silver per metric ton or 1,247 grams/tonne. That helped make this camp the second-largest primary silver producer in Canada, boasting one of the richest silver-lead-zinc vein deposits the world's ever mined. Production from this area generated more wealth than the Klondike, which itself was considered one of the richest placer gold districts globally.

But a lot of silver, even very high-grade silver, remains. And with a stable mining regime, the potential and prospects are quite attractive. The Yukon is currently home to one of the world's highest-grade silver mines, with several other highly prospective projects being advanced.

Northern British Columbia also has a long history of precious metals mining. As far back as 1861, Alexander "Buck" Choquette found gold, kicking off the Stikine Gold Rush. Not much gold was found, but it triggered activity in the area. Prospecting and exploration were intermittent for the next century but have flourished in the past couple of decades, thanks in part to new road and power infrastructure.

There have been several large discoveries of gold, silver, and copper in what's known today as the Golden Triangle, located in northwestern British Columbia. The Eskay Creek Mine, discovered in 1988, produced about 3.3 million gold ounces and 160 million silver ounces, both at extremely high grades. Today, there are several existing projects with high silver grades. Some are past producers, while others are looking to expand and restart former producing mines.

Now that you know where the best places are to mine silver, let's turn our attention to how silver is used.

I'll bet just how present silver is in our daily lives is going to surprise you.

Key Takeaways

- Jurisdiction matters in silver mining, favouring Canada, the U.S., Mexico, Australia, and some parts of Europe and South America.

- Mexico contributes 23% of global mined silver as the largest supplier.
- Parts of the U.S. and Canada have strong potential and favorable mining regimes.

Chapter 25: Silver's Demand Profile

Since my earlier days as a boy scout, I still have and cherish an iconic Swiss Army pocket knife my dad bought me. It's the kind with a lot of features like a magnifying glass, screw drivers, scissors, tweezers, a file, a saw, and even two bottle openers.

Silver reminds me a lot of that knife, because it's a multipurpose metal used in a vast number of ways, with new applications being developed frequently.

It can even help make it rain. I'm not kidding.

I was surprised to learn that silver is used in something called "cloud seeding." That's when airplanes release plumes of silver iodide, a crystalline material, that can modify the cloud's structure and cause it to rain or even snow. And the silver residue that falls to the ground is harmless.

Silver is the best conductor of heat and electricity. That makes it highly prized in electronic components like wiring, switches, and printed circuit boards. As one of the most reflective substances, silver has been used for centuries as backing for mirrors. Today, it's crucial in solar panels. Since it's both malleable and ductile, silver makes for beautiful jewelry and silverware. These same characteristics also make it ideal for micro-electronics like tablets and smartphones since it can be shaped and pressed into minute spaces without the risk of breaking.

In many cases, gold can serve the same purpose. But silver's advantage is its price. Of course, it's more costly than copper or nickel, but they don't have the same physical properties. What's more, often only very small amounts of silver are needed, like in smartphones, making the cost factor almost irrelevant to the overall production or retail cost.

As the green revolution takes hold and the world gravitates

towards green/clean energy and energy conservation, silver has a crucial role to play. That's because more silver is used in environmentally friendly technologies than in conventional ones. As a result, the Silver Institute expects that, within just four years, the first and second most important industrial demand sectors for silver will be solar and automotive.

Silver Demand

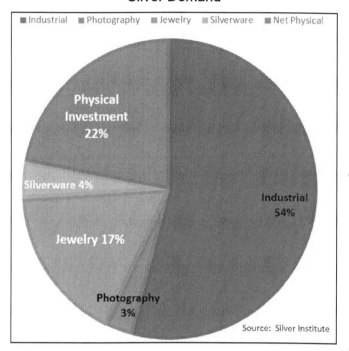

Source: Silver Institute World Silver Survey 2021

Silver in Medicine

Silver is exceptionally good at killing and limiting bacteria. This use reaches way back to when silver coins were placed in wine and water containers to preserve freshness. Today, it's used in countless water purifiers to prevent bacteria and algae growth. Many water purification systems in public pools, municipal water treatment and hospitals have silver ions added to fight contamination.

More recently, researchers discovered that silver is effective at penetrating the cell walls of bacteria, breaking down their inner chemical structures. And it accomplishes all this while leaving mammalian cells unaffected.

Silver nitrate was used for decades by doctors. To prevent infection, they would place drops of the silver compound in newborns' eyes. Silver foil and silver sutures were employed during World War I to treat battlefield wounds and deep wounds. That's lasted, with silver now commonly found in bandages and ointments. Unlike antibiotics, bacteria don't develop resistance to silver.

Today, silver continues to reveal ever more ways it can be used. It's embedded in medical equipment like breathing tubes, catheters, needles, stethoscopes and surgical tools, and it's applied to surfaces like door handles and furniture to kill bacteria and limit infections.

It's no exaggeration to say that silver saves lives.

Silver in Automobiles

If the car of the future doesn't need a driver or gasoline, you can thank silver for that too.

Silver's high thermal and electrical conductivity make it ideal to use in light vehicles. That means it's vital to navigation, infotainment, power steering, driver alertness systems, ABS, and other safety features. Silver's use in high-tech computer systems and battery technology means it's crucial to self-driving cars and electric vehicles.

Selected Automotive Electrical & Electronic Components & Applications

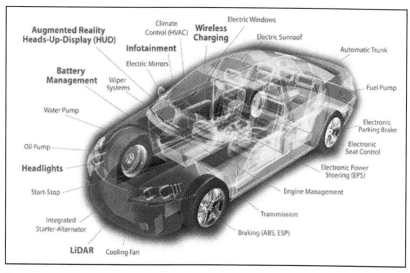

Source: The Silver Institute

According to the Silver Institute, silver demand from the automotive sector will be robust for several years into the future. Automotive silver requirements are currently about 60 million ounces annually but are forecast to rise by 50% to 90 million ounces by 2025.

Consider that traditional internal combustion engine vehicles use about 0.5-1.0 ounce (15-28 grams) of silver, hybrid vehicles demand 0.63-1.35 ounces (18-38 grams), and electric vehicles are up around 0.9-1.75 ounces (25-50 grams). Given the rapid rise in hybrid and electric vehicle adoption, silver demand growth from the automotive sector is likely to remain elevated.

Hybrid and EV Production Projection (Millions of Units)

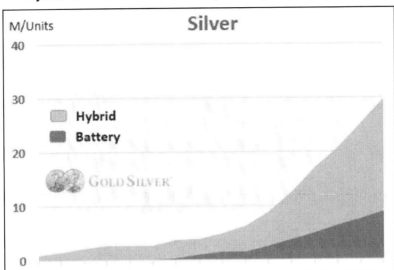

Source: goldsilver.com, LMC Automotive

Silver in Solar Panels

Photovoltaics, also known as solar panels, are the single largest industrial application for silver. Each year, this subsector alone consumes an impressive 100 million silver ounces. That's currently about 10% of the annual world silver supply, and it's expected to grow despite thrifting efforts.

Naturally, solar panel manufacturers are always looking to lower costs. One way is to reduce the silver content of each panel. But there are practical limits to cutting out silver. Substitution is another, but as I explained earlier, silver's reflexivity and conductivity are unmatched, making it the go-to metal for solar panels.

Thrifting has led to an 80% drop in the average quantity of silver required over the past decade. But the overall silver demand level has held around 100 million silver ounces for the past five years thanks to the growing demand for solar panels.

That has made photovoltaics the leading source of green electricity and the cheapest form of renewable energy. Solar installations are up 380-fold over the last 20 years.

Growth of Solar Installations vs. Silver Loadings, 2010 - 2021

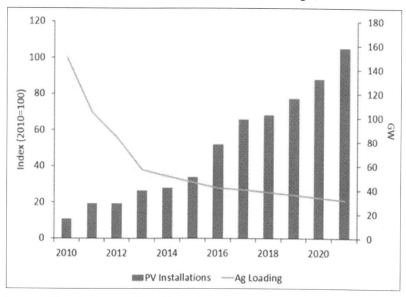

Source: Metals Focus, The Silver Institute

Projections for the growth of solar power are impressive. According to Facts & Factors Marketing Research, the global solar energy market in 2019 stood at $50 billion. They forecast a compound annual growth rate of 20%, expecting the global solar market to reach around $200 billion by 2026.

Thrifting may already be reaching its limits, as manufacturers are concerned about the compatibility and reliability of potential substitute materials. Together with expected growth, this suggests demand for silver from solar panels will remain very strong.

Silver in Photography

Around 1800 British photographer Thomas Wedgwood used paper treated with silver nitrate to capture images. From there, constant improvements were made by others, each advancing photography with silver compounds.

Traditional film photography has all but disappeared for most consumers. Today, a majority of professionals have also moved to digital photography as the quality, flexibility, and convenience have improved. As a result, silver demand from this sector has fallen dramatically over recent decades and is now less than half its level of ten years ago. The Silver Institute reports that global photographic demand was 61.6 million ounces in 2011 but dropped to 27.6 million ounces by 2020.

Still, there's a resurgence of interest in using "old-school," silver-based instant photography like Polaroid cameras and 35mm film. And some commercial movies still use silver-based films for their ability to capture fine detail and color. As well, developing countries still use silver-based X-Rays due to lower costs.

Silver in Electronics

Electronics is another demand sector where silver is indispensable.

Look around you. You've probably got a smartphone, tablet, laptop or desktop computer, or flat-screen TV nearby. Many of us have several of these. And that's just on the consumer side.

Think of commercial, industrial, medical, and military electronic equipment around the world.

Most of these modern devices use silver, even if it's a tiny amount. That's why silver can be found practically everywhere. And it's why nearly one-third (32.5%) of the global silver supply finds its way into electronics.

Precious Metals Volume into Electronic Markets

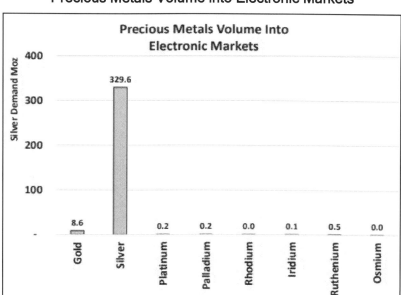

Source: Silver Institute, Precious Metals Commodity Management LLC

On/off buttons (membrane switches) common to most electronic devices use silver since it can deliver millions of cycles reliably. The metal's superb electrical conductivity makes it ideal for printed circuit boards found across the electronics sector. RFID tags, used to track inventory and prevent theft, use silver-based inks and films.

Demand for silver in printed and flexible electronics is about 48 million ounces annually. The Silver Institute forecasts demand will rise to about 74 million ounces by 2030, absorbing 615 million ounces of silver through the decade. As technology becomes increasingly commonplace in daily lives around the world, printed and flexible electronics will play a more prominent role. Wearable electronics like smartwatches, appliances, medical devices, and internet-connected gadgets are exploding in use. Sensors for light, motion, temperature, and moisture all employ printed and flexible electronics.

So, it's natural that the electronics subsector promises to have the fastest growing demand profile for industrial silver usage.

Silver in Jewelry and Silverware

Silver has long been prized for jewelry going back millennia.

Around 3,500 BC, people living in modern-day Turkey were the first to extract silver from lead. They used it to create decorative items, but few have survived or been found.

Early Egyptians also prized silver. And since pure silver had to be imported, it was worth *more than gold* and used exclusively for the highest-ranking members of society.

To this day, silver remains noted for its luster, workability, and more accessible pricing, making it a popular choice for fashion jewelry. Although pure silver is considered 99.9% silver or 0.999 fineness, it's typically alloyed with other metals to harden and strengthen it. Copper is most used to form "sterling silver," which is 7.5% copper and 92.5% silver.

Also known as 925 silver, sterling has been the standard worldwide for centuries. Its resilience makes for superb rings, bracelets, charms, and necklaces. This is especially true in India and East Asia, which together represent about 65% of global silver jewelry demand.

Silverware has long been popular, with sterling silver the standard fineness used in hollowware and flatware since the 1300s. It's fashioned into bowls, vases, cutlery, decanters, and candlesticks. Many of us have heard the expression "born with a silver spoon," which means to be born into a wealthy family.

But the phrase is thought to hearken back to the late 18th century. That's when godparents gifted silver spoons to their godchildren, and British royals dined using silverware. Babies fed with silver spoons back then were thought to be healthier than those who used utensils made from other materials. Silver's antibacterial properties probably contributed to the term and likely did help keep many babies safer from infections. Today, silverware represents about 6% of silver demand, with most of that coming from India.

Silver's Emerging Applications

The Silver Institute's World Silver Survey 2021 highlights three new and emerging uses for silver.

One of these is cold sintering silver powder. That's when small silver particles are compressed together. Their better thermal and conductive properties allow silver to improve and enable technologies, like in semiconductors, where lead soldering may be replaced by cold sintered silver.

Many applications require lower temperature soldering, particularly wireless communication, medical, automotive, aerospace and aviation, as they've dealt with fatigue and failure issues. As well, cold sintered silver offers the advantage of being processed on a smaller footprint without moving, making for more precise control. This also helps minimize the effects of heat on other sensitive components. Silver sintering's superb optical transparency, conductivity and flexibility make it ideal for solar cells, displays and touch screens while using less energy and aiding the environment.

5G cellular communication technology is another innovation that's both a beneficiary of - and a "trigger" for - silver.

And it's an innovation I'll be watching closely in the months and years to come.

Small-cell base stations should outnumber those in 4G networks by 40-60 times, multiplying the need for multiple-input/multiple-output (MIMO) antennae and switch contacts in relays and inverters. This, combined with the more widespread Internet of

Things (IoT) for cars, healthcare, agriculture and connected cities, will help push silver demand much higher.

Induction charging, such as the wireless charging that we see in electric toothbrushes, smartphones, and smartwatches, is on the rise as consumers move towards frequent wireless charging. Vehicle charging may be next, but certain issues still need to be overcome. Induction charging is currently less efficient than plug-in charging and paying for the infrastructure for vehicle charging is another issue. But these challenges will be resolved and lead to much wider adoption, furthering the demand for silver.

Silver Investment

In my view, silver investment will be the wildcard factor that will help drive overall demand for the metal much higher in the next several years. It's probably the most underrated and misunderstood aspect of silver demand.

I see two big reasons for this. First, silver bugs are wild about silver. I mean, they really love their silver. I get it. I too love silver. For some, it seems to nearly border on cult.

The other big reason is related. Sentiment plays such a huge role in investing, yet it's one of its least understood aspects. I think that's especially true for a relatively small market like silver, whose fans are very committed...and driven. I'll go into more detail on this later.

In my experience, years of researching, investing, and tracking silver markets can help provide a "feel" for sentiment. It's part art and part science. There are multiple technical indicators that suggest potential strength, weakness, or neutrality for silver and silver investments over particular time frames. And some aspects can't be measured. Instead, living and breathing this market can give one a sense of what may lie ahead in the near, medium, and longer terms.

I expect many strong demand years ahead, in part because of developments in the silver investment markets in 2019, but especially during 2020 and early 2021.

By now, you already know that silver's been a proven investment vehicle not only for centuries but for millennia. And given the macroeconomic outlook, I expect silver to take on an even more important investment role going forward.

Thanks to Modern Monetary Theory, we're in an environment where interest rates are being kept artificially low - down near zero - for years, while currencies are being dramatically diluted through printing. In fact, I'm impressed at the rate at which investors, in general, are realizing this and acting.

But as I explained earlier, silver is a minuscule market compared to other traditional investments like stocks, bonds, and even gold. That means relatively little buying can drive outsized price gains.

When we look at silver investment, there are basically two main sources of demand. The first is physical demand in the form of bars and coins. That's when people buy these items from bullion dealers or other suppliers.

The second is demand from the Exchange Traded Funds (ETF) sector. ETFs hold silver on behalf of investors in the form of 1,000 oz. bars, which are also known as commercial bars. However, ETFs are like equities traded on stock markets. That makes them easy to buy and sell. And their 1,000 oz. bars can be taken as physical delivery by larger investors or even industrial consumers who might melt them down to use them.

Because most of these bars simply remain in vaults and have not been converted into coins or smaller bars, many industry researchers do not include ETF demand as part of physical silver demand.

I disagree with this approach since silver buying tends to be "sticky." This means that typically, once investors buy physical or ETF silver, they tend to hold onto it and are reluctant to sell. From my perspective, once silver is acquired by an ETF, it tends to be removed from the overall silver supply. This tendency has been observed for more than a decade. And in the past few years, it has intensified.

That's why, in my view, not including silver ETF demand as part of overall demand provides an unrealistic picture of the silver market. Instead, including it can lead to major shifts in the supply/demand balance.

Let's look at the numbers from the Silver Institute's World Silver Survey 2022.

Silver Supply and Demand
World Silver Survey 2022, The Silver Institute

Silver Supply and Demand											Year on Year	
Million ounces	2013	2014	2015	2016	2017	2018	2019	2020	2021	2022F	2021	2022F
Supply												
Mine Production	845.3	882.1	896.9	900.0	863.7	850.2	835.9	781.1	822.6	843.2	5%	2%
Recycling	180.3	181.3	147.3	145.9	147.2	148.6	147.7	165.2	173.0	180.5	7%	4%
Net Hedging Supply	-	10.7	2.2	-	-	-	15.2	8.5	-	6.0	na	na
Net Official Sector Sales	1.7	1.2	1.1	1.1	1.0	1.2	1.0	1.2	1.8	1.5	28%	1%
Total Supply	1,027.3	1,055.3	1,047.4	1,046.9	1,011.9	1,000.0	999.8	953.0	997.2	1,030.3	5%	3%
Demand												
Industrial	449.6	438.9	441.1	475.3	503.6	499.6	498.1	464.9	508.2	529.6	9%	6%
...of which photovoltaics	50.5	48.4	54.1	93.7	101.8	92.5	98.7	101.0	113.7	127.0	13%	12%
Photography	45.8	43.6	41.2	37.8	35.1	33.8	32.7	27.8	28.7	28.4	3%	-1%
Jewelry	186.9	192.9	201.7	188.4	195.2	201.9	200.3	149.8	181.4	201.8	21%	11%
Silverware	46.5	53.6	57.9	53.9	59.6	67.6	62.1	32.4	42.7	52.7	32%	23%
Net Physical Investment	300.6	283.1	310.4	212.0	155.7	165.2	186.8	205.0	278.7	279.2	36%	0%
Net Hedging Demand	29.3	-	-	12.0	2.1	7.7	-	-	9.4	-	na	na
Total Demand	1,058.7	1,012.4	1,052.3	979.4	951.3	975.7	980.0	880.0	1,040.0	1,101.8	18%	5%
Market Balance	-31.4	43.2	-5.0	67.5	60.6	24.3	19.8	73.0	-51.8	-71.5	na	38%
Net Investment in ETPs	4.7	-0.3	-17.1	53.9	7.2	-21.4	83.3	331.1	64.9	25.0	-80%	-62%
Market Balance less ETPs	-36.2	43.5	12.1	13.6	53.5	45.7	-63.4	-258.1	-116.7	-96.5	-55%	-17%
Silver Price (US$/oz, London price)	23.79	19.08	15.68	17.14	17.05	15.71	16.21	20.55	25.14	23.90	22%	-5%

Source: World Silver Survey 2022, The Silver Institute, Metals Focus

As you can see from the table above, which I've highlighted, Net Physical Investment in 2020 was 205 million ounces. That contributed to total silver demand of 880 million ounces and a market surplus of 73 million ounces. However, Net Investment in ETPs (ETPs are Exchange Traded Products, another name for Exchange Traded Funds) was 331 million ounces. Given that total supply was 953 million ounces for 2020, ETP demand alone represented more than one-third of the entire year's supply. *Yet this amount is left out of Total Demand and is listed separately.*

When included, however, in Market Balance less ETPs, *the silver market was 258 million ounces in deficit.* That represents more than 27% of the entire supply of silver for 2020. And still, this figure is shown separately.

Although 2020 may have been an exceptional year, here's another point to consider. Adding together Net Physical Investment of 205 million ounces with Net Investment in ETPs (331Moz) produces a total of 536 million ounces. And that represents 56% of the 953 million ounces of supply. So, **more than half of all silver supply for 2020 went to physical investment and ETPs**: an astounding fact.

According to the Silver Institute and BMO Capital markets, Solar and 5G telecommunication technologies, along with physical investment, will be the fastest-growing sectors of silver demand over the next decade.

Silver Demand Contribution by End-Use Forecast

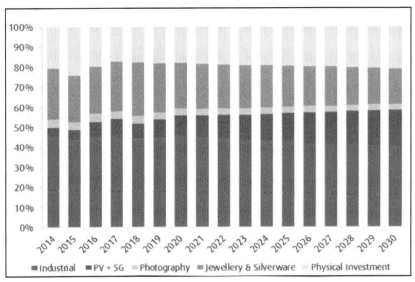

Source: Silver Institute, BMO Capital Markets

With all the forecast demand from solar, automotive, industrial and investment, ongoing supply shortfalls are expected over the next several years. And that deficit is set to multiply from there.

Silver Demand Forecast to 2050

Silver Demand - High Case

Legend: Semiconductor, Consumer Electronics, Other Electronic, Power distribution, Solar PV, Automotive, Brazing Alloys, Other Industrial (EO), Photography, Jewelry, Silverware, Net Physical Investment, - - - Mined, - - - Mined + Recycle

Zero Emissions Powertrain + 100% IRENA Renewables

Source: Precious Metals Commodity Management

Unless miners and recyclers grow their supply aggressively, the impending silver shortage will be huge.

And that's likely to set a rising floor under silver prices.

Key Takeaways

- Silver's use in high tech and green energy is soaring, with solar panels consuming 10% of supply.

- Silver is crucial in medicine for its anti-bacterial properties.

- Silver investment is likely to be the most influential factor driving prices higher.

Chapter 26: The Key New Silver Investment Trends

In many ways, silver never stands still. I just showed you a host of new uses and applications that are continually being developed.

But I also want you to know about several trends emerging in the realm of silver investing.

Some are not completely new, but they are gaining steam and becoming more significant. Others are very recent yet have the potential to add considerable demand for physical silver. Even if some of these don't pan out, it's important to know and factor in their potential to add pressure to silver's already very tight market conditions.

One of these promising areas is cryptocurrencies.

We all know Bitcoin as the first and dominant cryptocurrency. Bitcoin will keep facing challenges as some governments disparage and regulate it, while others try outright bans of one form or another. I don't think that will be successful. High-profile money managers, tech entrepreneurs and even banks have gotten on board, many reversing their earlier doubts.

Bitcoin is decentralized, the blockchain is verified by more than 100,000 independent nodes globally, and it has a limited supply of 21 million coins. Other cryptocurrencies and central banks may want in on this sector, but there will only ever be one Bitcoin.

Bitcoin has come a long way. Today, it's gained not only the acceptance of prominent investors like Paul Tudor Jones, Ray Dalio, and Elon Musk, but it's also been integrated into several well-established payment systems. MassMutual, the 170-year-old insurance giant, bought $100 million of bitcoin in 2020. In early 2021, electric carmaker Tesla announced it had purchased $1.5 billion worth.

And crypto as a sector is exploding. PayPal said it was investing heavily into a new business unit aimed exclusively at cryptocurrencies. Their idea is to facilitate cryptocurrency payments across PayPal's network. It's all part of a burgeoning trend called decentralized finance, or DeFi.

An incredible 29 million merchants use PayPal. They will be able to accept cryptocurrency payments through that network. In fact, to simplify things, PayPal will automatically convert crypto payments into the national currency of the merchant.

The main advantage for merchants is the speed of transaction clearing. Credit card and bank payments typically take 24 hours or longer to settle. With crypto, that will happen within minutes or even seconds, allowing merchants to access their funds much sooner.

Recently, Visa (credit cards) announced it would allow customers to use the USD Coin cryptocurrency to settle transactions on its network. USD Coin is a "stable coin cryptocurrency" whose value is pegged to the U.S. dollar. This follows on the heels of Mastercard, BlackRock and BNY Mellon, all confirming they would be facilitating cryptocurrency transactions for investments and payments.

Despite all this, some challenges remain.

Many people can't get past the idea that there's nothing physical backing Bitcoin. And if you have no electricity or internet access, you can't get at your crypto.

Central Bank Digital Currencies

The fact that nothing physical is backing most cryptos is not that different from the currency we use today. It has value because central banks say so, and people accept it. So that's not the biggest hurdle. However, if there is a large and extended power or internet outage, there's a real problem as crypto is accessed on a computer, tablet, or smartphone.

But these challenges haven't stopped numerous central banks from researching and implementing digital currencies. The next chart shows how central banks worldwide have been busy developing their own central bank digital currencies (CBDCs).

Central Banks Ranked by Maturity of Retail Digital Currency Development, April 2021

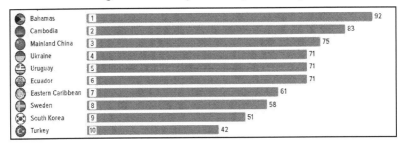

Source: U.S. Global Investors

Over 80 central banks are currently working on this, so CBDCs are coming soon to a country near you.

In early 2022, China was testing its own CBDC - dubbed the e-CNY - in several major cities, allowing visitors to use it at the Beijing Winter Olympics. Around the same time, India announced it would launch its own CBDC.

Together, the populations of China and India total 2.8 billion. That means 35% of the world will soon live under a CBDC financial system.

There are over 400 million people in China and India without a bank account. "Unbanked" people would have easier access to tax refunds or stimulus checks. According to the South China Morning Post, China is on its way to becoming the first cashless society by implementing the "digital yuan."

Don't think the U.S. is willing to be left behind. In February 2021, U.S. Federal Reserve Chair Jerome Powell said a digital USD is a "high-priority project...We are looking very carefully, very carefully, at the question of whether we should issue a digital dollar." Around the same time, Treasury Secretary Janet Yellen told the New York Times, "It makes sense for central banks to be looking at" CBDCs, adding that "too many Americans don't have access to easy payments systems and banking accounts, and I think this is something that a digital dollar, a central bank digital currency, could help with."

But CBDCs are not the same as some cryptocurrencies. Bitcoin has a hard supply limit of 21 million coins and stands for the free market and decentralization. CBDCs are the exact opposite, representing centralization with no supply limits. Central banks are concerned about losing their role as the sole issuer and controller of currency. The level of control CBDCs will ultimately give central planners will be unmatched. And the COVID-19 pandemic has massively accelerated this trend.

Central banks love the idea of eliminating cash. CBDCs will allow them to track every currency unit they create. That way, they know who spends how much, when, where and on what. It also gives them the ability to freeze accounts and impose negative interest rates, effectively taxing cash holdings with minimal effort.

An article in *The Telegraph* discussed the future of CBDCs in the U.K. It pointed out that the Bank of England called on ministers to intervene on programming:

> *"Digital cash could be programmed to ensure it is only spent on essentials, or goods which an employer or government deems to be sensible.*

The Bank of England has called on ministers to decide whether a central bank digital currency should be "programmable," ultimately giving the issuer control over how it is spent by the recipient."

CBDCs can be created and distributed much more easily and quickly than existing currencies. This is another serious concern in my view (think inflation), but a major advantage if you're a central planner.

Already, the world has reached an astounding $289 trillion in total global debt, or more than 360% of world GDP. I expect CBDCs will be adopted, and they will surely boost debts levels even further and faster.

Combining CBDCs with Modern Monetary Theory will greatly accelerate the death of the dollar.

Silver-Backed Crypto

According to 2020's *In Gold We Trust* report, there are already over 70 gold-backed cryptocurrencies, and several silver-backed ones.

As the market does what markets do, many will likely fail. Still, they expect some leaders will emerge, become more widely accepted, and establish a new asset class.

I believe precious metals will have a major role to play in any true reset of the financial system. Even if I'm wrong on that point, they're still going to soar as inflation and chaos hedges.

In fact, I think we will ultimately have a gold and/or silver-backed cryptocurrency that may even be government-mandated once faith in fiat currencies is completely lost. That new currency will have both intrinsic value and the conveniences of cryptocurrency. And if that currency is on a blockchain that logs all transactions, it can also be very secure.

Imagine silver and gold, the world's true money since millennia, being transferred instantly between parties. That's 24/7, no wait, no borders, and at negligible cost. It's hard not to see this in our future.

There are already several cryptocurrencies backed by precious metals or that are in the development stages. One of the main advantages of this approach to holding precious metals is that it allows ownership of small quantities without dealing with storage issues while offering security and the ability to transfer value easily and quickly. In many ways, it's like the evolution of precious metals-backed Exchange Traded Funds (ETFs).

Here are a few companies that are active in this space. Aurus (aurus.io), for example, has built a platform allowing refiners, distributors, and vaults to autonomously tokenize precious metals. There are other similar developments:

- **deVere Group** has the **Pax Gold** crypto, which is backed by a portion of a London Good Delivery gold bar.

- **Dignity Gold** company has secured $6 billion in gold from mining claims in Nevada and Arizona for its **DIGau** digital token.

- **Lode** (https://lode.one/) has the **AUX Coin** which represents 1 milligram of vaulted, audited, insured and verifiable gold bullion, while the **AGX Coin** represents 1 gram of silver.

- **Kinesis** is an entire ecosystem consisting of an online cryptocurrency and fiat exchange, the **KAU** gold-backed (1 gram gold) cryptocurrency and the **KAG** silver-backed (1 ounce silver) cryptocurrency, as well as a prepaid Visa debit card and even the Kinesis cold digital asset wallet.

(**Note**: I've provided the above for informational purposes only. I am not endorsing any of these companies).

Even if precious metals-backed cryptocurrencies don't replace CBDCs, they are exciting as they may go a long way to solving the problems of storage, security, and rapid transferability.

This is an area of precious metals to watch closely. People may gravitate towards this as they seek a convenient store of value based on one of the oldest forms of real money: gold and silver.

And this could be a burgeoning new source of demand for precious metals, helping to push silver much higher in the future. If we head in that direction, producers and refiners would have a ready market for their physical silver.

Regaining Monetary Status

While mostly the exception, a few places in the world don't charge tax on certain forms of gold and/or silver. These include Norway, the United Kingdom and Singapore. Within the European Union, certain recognized gold coins and bullion products are exempt from taxes, but that's not the case for silver.

In the U.S., there has been a movement in recent years to repeal taxes on the sale of gold, silver and in some cases also platinum and palladium bullion coins and bars. The **Sound Money Defense League** has often spearheaded this movement, supported by others including Money Metals Exchange, Campaign for Liberty, and representatives of coin dealers.

Their tireless work has been paying off. There are currently 42 U.S. states which have removed some or all sales taxes from gold and silver. State legislatures have come to understand the logical reasons these metals should be free from taxes. JP Cortez is Policy Director at the Sound Money Defense League, which, as per their website is, "a non-partisan national public policy organization working to restore sound money on the state and federal level."

In testimony before House and Senate Committees in Ohio, Cortez explained why so many states have chosen to remove some or all sales taxes from gold and silver:

- **Taxing precious metals is unfair to certain savers and investors:** Gold and silver are held as forms of savings and investment. States do not tax the purchase of stocks, bonds, ETFs, currencies, and other financial instruments, so it makes no sense to tax monetary metals.

- **Levying sales taxes on precious metals is illogical because gold and silver are inherently held for resale:** Sales taxes are typically levied on final consumer goods. Precious metals are inherently held for resale, not "consumption," making the application of sales taxes on precious metals illogical and especially inappropriate.

- **Taxing gold and silver harms in-state businesses:** it's a competitive marketplace, so buyers in states with precious-metals sales taxes often take their business to neighboring states that have eliminated or reduced sales tax on precious metals. Investors can easily avoid paying $136.50 in sales taxes, for example, on a $1,950 purchase of a one-ounce gold bar. Therefore, levying sales tax on precious metals harms in-state businesses, who will lose business to out-of-state precious metals dealers. Coin conventions also tend to avoid the sales tax states.

- **Taxing precious metals is harmful to citizens attempting to protect their assets:** Purchasers of precious metals aren't fat-cat investors. Most who buy physical precious metals do so in small increments as a way of saving money. Precious metals investors are purchasing precious metals to preserve their wealth against the damaging effects of inflation. Inflation especially harms "the little guy" - including pensioners, retirees on fixed incomes, wage-earners, and savers.

But this is only a first step towards reclaiming silver and gold as money. Some efforts go beyond the removal of sales taxes. States such as Utah, Wyoming and Oklahoma have gone further, recognizing gold and silver bullion as legal tender. Remember, the U.S. Constitution allows states to give their citizens the right to settle debts in silver and gold. Article I, Section 10 says, "No State shall…make any Thing but gold and silver Coin a Tender in Payment of Debts."

Several U.S. states have similar goals, with some advancing legislation to recognize silver and gold as legal tender, and to remove capital gains taxes. In many ways, it only makes sense. After all, national mints often produce silver and gold bullion coins with various denominations, making them legal tender for the payment of debts. If Federal Reserve Notes, better known as cash, are not subject to taxes, then it stands to reason that silver and gold should not be either. It may be a long road ahead, but encouraging progress is being made.

Be Your Own Central Bank

In 2020 **MicroStrategy (NYSE: MSTR)**, led by Chairman and CEO Michael Saylor, was the first public company to invest a sizeable portion of its treasury assets in Bitcoin.

That shocked the markets. And yet it was a simple strategy to diversify and protect the buying power of MicroStrategy's surplus cash: half a billion dollars' worth.

Then, in early 2021, high-profile entrepreneur Elon Musk of **Tesla (Nasdaq: TSLA)** fame decided to plow $1.5 billion of the company's cash into bitcoin. The move drew a lot of attention.

Around that time, Tesla's 10-k filing said:

> *In January 2021, we updated our investment policy to provide us with more flexibility to further diversify and maximize returns on our cash that is not required to maintain adequate operating liquidity. As part of the policy, which was duly approved by the Audit Committee of our Board of Directors,* **we may invest a portion of such cash in certain alternative reserve assets including digital assets, gold bullion, gold exchange-traded funds, and other assets as specified in the future.** *(Emphasis mine)*

That's when it struck me; many corporations, especially large multinationals, sit on billions, and in some cases, hundreds of billions in cash. In early 2021 Alphabet's (Google's) pile was $137 billion, Microsoft's was $132 billion, Apple had $77 billion, Amazon $84 billion, and Facebook was sitting on $62 billion.

That was half a trillion dollars...just amongst these five.

I thought to myself, if we go through an extended period of high inflation, these and other companies may one day be challenged by their shareholders for holding too much cash as it loses purchasing power, hurting share values.

Corporations, pension funds and insurance companies - anyone responsible to stakeholders - could one day face class-action lawsuits if they don't diversify into inflation-fighting reserve assets. It's not beyond the realm of possibility, especially in today's litigious-happy world.

Maybe that's at least one reason so many have resorted to stock buybacks. We know several have borrowed, at historically low interest rates, to do this. From management's perspective, at least, it's a no-brainer. But is it really in shareholders' best interest?

Yet, the attraction to precious metals for inflation protection is regaining prominence. In mid-2020, the Ohio Police & Fire Pension Fund approved a 5% allocation into gold. It was a move made for the exact reasons I just mentioned: to diversify its portfolio and hedge against the risk of inflation. Wilshire Associates, the fund's investment consultant, made the recommendation.

A few years back, Shayne McGuire, Director of Global Research, launched and managed a gold fund for the Teacher Retirement System of Texas. He said:

> *"Before 2008, counterparty risk was not a consideration if you had the backing of Lehman Brothers or Citigroup or even the largest bank, RBS, or the backing of a colossal insurance company like AIG. Gold is ultimate financial insurance, the only viable and liquid investment asset that is not another entity's liability and pension funds are talking about this.*

> *"In this regard, a renowned natural resources entrepreneur with a strong historical take on the gold market shared this thought with me last week: 'Just as the prudent man rule would have prohibited asset managers with a fiduciary responsibility from owning gold* **just a decade ago, one day we are likely to see the exact opposite. Everyone will need to own some gold**

in their portfolio, which will have notable
consequences for the price of gold in the
future.'" (Emphasis mine)

There's even a connection to U.S. states working to have silver and gold accepted as legal tender. In early 2022, Idaho passed House Bill 522, The Idaho Sound Money Reserves Act, with overwhelming support.

As per the Sound Money Defense League, which supported the bill, it "would permit - but not require - the State Treasurer to hold some portion of state funds in physical gold and silver to help secure state assets against the risks of inflation and financial turmoil and/or to achieve capital gains as measured in Federal Reserve Notes."

The bill was introduced by Representative Ron Nate (R-Rexburg), who commented, "Idaho's current investments are comprised almost entirely of debt instruments with a negative real yield, plus they have a default risk. That's risk without reward. We need to give our Treasurer another tool in the toolbox, the option to hold gold and silver, to protect taxpayer funds."

The League's policy director, JP Cortez, explained that "Inflation has reached every Idaho home to the tune of at least 7%, which means that the real annual rate of return for Idaho taxpayers on its $10 billion in 'idle moneys' is deeply negative, perhaps greater than $500 million."

The next step is to seek approval at the Senate level.

In partnership with the World Gold Council, a research survey by Greenwich Associates noted that gold is expected to become increasingly important to institutional investors.

Andrew McCollum, head of investment management at

Greenwich said, "The results from the study show that, in addition to the now decade-old quest to meet return targets in a low-yield environment, institutional investors face a new set of challenges as they position portfolios for the post-COVID-19 period. Among the most important: the need to protect their portfolios from mounting inflationary risks."

The survey results indicated that one in five investors have an allocation to gold. Amongst those, 38% are planning to increase their allocation within three years. Almost 40% of non-gold investors intend to establish a position in the metal, with the average amount being about 4% of their portfolio. Most of these investors appreciate all three features of gold - inflation protection, diversification, and risk-adjusted return enhancement - as important reasons to include the metal in their portfolios.

The winds of change are blowing. Pension, corporate, and even government fund managers are looking for alternative reserve assets. These managers will soon be expected to include prudent silver and gold holdings in their portfolios.

Central banks own hundreds - even thousands - of tons of gold as a reserve asset. Although they downplay and disparage the metal, they know the crucial role it plays. By owning some silver, you become your own central bank. Silver is an asset, unlike a stock or bond, that depends on no one else to honor it.

One thing is sure. Silver and gold have proven themselves as the ultimate reserve assets and financial insurance over millennia. And they're set to fulfill that role once again.

Key Takeaways

- As money becomes digital, silver-backed cryptocurrencies could have a role to play.

- Efforts are ongoing to recognize silver as money, seeking the removal of taxes on purchases and capital gains.

- Corporations and even governments are looking to plow cash reserves into precious metals to protect against inflation.

In **Part III**, I showed you that, despite being close cousins, silver and gold do have important differences that go well beyond their prices.

The silver market is about one-tenth the size of the gold market. Nearly 90% of gold is for investment, while just 10% is used in industry. On the other hand, about 50% of silver is used in industry and, depending on how it's calculated, up to 40% of silver is bought for investment.

Thanks to Mother Nature, only about 27% of silver is mined as a primary metal. Most silver is extracted along with other metals like gold, copper, lead, and zinc. That makes silver supply *inelastic*, so its supply does not rise substantially even when prices do.

Only a handful of countries produce most mined silver, and supply has been falling on balance for the last several years. As a "wonder metal", silver has countless uses in medicine, automobiles, solar panels, photography, electronics, jewelry and silverware, and emerging high-tech applications.

Industrial consumption is growing steadily yet rapidly, but investment in physical silver and ETFs has been the wildcard factor for demand. The COVID-19 pandemic and social media events triggered silver-buying frenzies. That's led to total silver ETF holdings surpassing annual supply, and premiums on physical coins reaching triple normal levels.

I believe the next global financial reset could lead to big demand for silver-backed cryptocurrencies, several of which already exist. Meanwhile, there are efforts in different jurisdictions to remove taxes on physical silver and gold. I believe silver will become a corporate reserve asset as more people come to realize how quickly their cash is losing purchasing power to inflation.

Silver is unique in many ways. In **Part IV** you're about to see how it has consistently outperformed other assets, including gold, in bull markets.

Silver is a relatively small market, many investors enthusiastically embrace it, and it's still amazingly cheap compared to other metals.

For all these reasons, silver has one of the most compelling outlooks of any asset. With that in mind, I'll give you my forecast for a peak silver price. At first glance it will sound outlandish. But when you see how I reach my conclusion, you'll understand that it may not be so crazy after all.

Let's explore what really makes silver tick, and how those factors can ignite hefty gains from silver - the metal, and silver-related investments like funds, developers, and explorers.

Part IV
Silver: Unique and Set to Soar

Introduction: What Drives the Silver Market

I have big plans for this book - and for you.

I want you to better understand the silver market. And that means you need to have a pretty good feel for the metal's historical, economic, and political backdrop.

Most important of all, I will show you how compelling investing in silver is today.

The goal: to spotlight the massive profit potential offered by this very special metal, and to demonstrate how you can grab your share of those gains.

I will detail how - because of Modern Monetary Theory - everyday currencies have moved away from being backed by silver and gold. The last year American coins had any silver in them was 1964, and in 1971 U.S. President Richard Nixon cut the dollar's last tie to gold.

Since then, the U.S. dollar, the world's *de facto* reserve currency, has been backed only by the full faith and credit of the U.S. government. It is, essentially, a matter of trust: a promise. The bottom line is the dollar is worth something only as long as others want it. That's true of all fiat currencies.

People are waking up to the fact that money has been created out of thin air for decades, especially after President Nixon closed the gold window.

Dollar creation got its next big boost when stocks peaked in 2000. Central planners increased the money supply to cushion stock market weakness and lessen recession risk. Next came the Great Financial Crisis of 2008-2009, when Modern Monetary Theory was put into practice - and never stopped. Most recently, it's been the global COVID-19 coronavirus pandemic that has pushed money printing into overdrive.

The thing is more and more people are catching on and realizing how their purchasing power is being eroded. Investors are fleeing cash, and that's why stocks in early 2022 were pushed to near all-time highs. That's why food prices have been climbing. It's why housing and other forms of real estate have been soaring.

Investors are seeking the shelter of hard assets to protect them from their debasing currency.

And yet, there are still big opportunities for investors who can spot them.

And one of the biggest is silver. This metal goes through huge bull markets. And those market runs are preceded by very specific, unique signals.

And I know what those signals are.

In **Part IV**, I'll show you what silver has done in previous bull markets. You'll see what's next for silver, silver stocks and other silver-related investment plays. You'll also see just how much wealth you can generate by investing in silver.

Silver is constantly compared with, and measured against, gold.

That's normal. Gold is the king of precious metals. But silver is the prime minister.

There's really nothing quite like silver. It's exceptional -- not only in its physical properties but also in its market properties. The psychology of how people buy, hold, and sell silver has a profound effect on its price action. If you understand this, you'll cash in on a tremendous opportunity.

There are numerous tools and indicators to help you know where silver stands on a historical and a relative basis. I'll work through these, so you know exactly when silver is cheap, fairly valued, or expensive.

I'll show you *what* market forces affect silver prices and *how* they affect them. I'll even give you my target for a peak silver price, the multiple ways I get there, and why I think it's totally achievable.

Let's start by looking at previous silver bull markets.

Chapter 27: Past is Prologue – The Silver Roadmap

With a good perspective on history, we can have a better understanding of the past and present, and thus a clear vision of the future."

CARLOS SLIM HELU,
MEXICAN BUSINESS MAGNATE

Silver enjoyed a massive secular bull market from about 1971 until 1980 and another major bull from about 2001 until 2011.

Most secular bull markets reach a period, usually about halfway on the time scale, where the commodity's price falls by roughly 50%, sometimes more. This is an observation by legendary commodities investor Jim Rogers.

In my own experience, this is often the case, but sometimes the price correction is less severe if it's drawn out over a longer period. Corrections are typically short and deep, or long and shallow. There is no rule, and it's never the same.

Let's dig into these previous bull markets to give us an idea of how silver has behaved. This will provide a roadmap for what may lie ahead. Spoiler alert: looking back on how silver performed in the past points to much bigger gains ahead.

In the 1970s, silver rose from a low near $1.30 in 1971 to a $50 peak in 1980. That produced a whopping 37 times gain or 3,700%. Every $1,000 invested in silver at $1.30 in 1971 was worth $38,000 at the peak in 1980. That's a testament to the massive potential silver bull markets offer.

Then, silver entered a long bear market and eventually bottomed in 2001 at $4.14. That's when it began a new bull, rising all the way back to $49 in 2011. Investors who had positioned themselves early enjoyed a 1,180% return.

Now let's dissect both of these bull markets in more detail, because understanding how they behaved can help you better prepare.

As you'll see, silver is volatile. But if you want to benefit from its big gains, you have to be willing to hold on through what is sometimes a wild ride.

1970s Silver Bull

As I said, silver bottomed near $1.30 in October 1971. That's when its 1970s secular bull market began.

Silver Price Performance 1971 - 1980

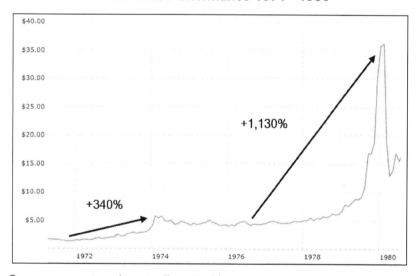

Source: macrotrends.net, silverstockinvestor.com

It first peaked at $5.78 in February 1974. That was a 340% gain in less than 3½ years. But then silver started to lose ground.

That correction took it from $5.78 in 1974 to $3.97 in January 1976. It was a relatively shallow but drawn-out correction. By

October 1978, silver had surpassed $5.78 and eventually reached a blow-off mania high at $50 in January 1980, gaining 1,160% from its 1976 low. (Note that the $50 high in 1980 doesn't appear in the above chart because it shows monthly prices).

Silver's gain from the 1971 low of $1.31 to its $50 1980 high was *an astounding 3,740%.*

Two decades later, it would do something similar.

2000s Silver Bull

In November 2001, silver bottomed at $4.14. Almost no one was paying attention, and practically no one wanted it. Silver was the perfect contrarian trade.

It then launched into a new bull market, rising to $19.89 by February 2008, producing a 380% gain.

Silver Price Performance 2001 - 2011

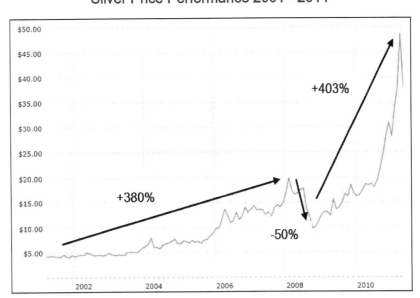

Source: macrotrends.net, silverstockinvestor.com

Silver then corrected from $19.89 to $9.73 in October 2008, putting in a relatively short-but-sharp 50% correction. This was the textbook 50% drawdown that Jim Rogers says to look out for. (By the way, 50% is approximate, and it sometimes plays out this way).

It then soared all the way to $49, reaching that level in April 2011, for a 403% gain from its 2008 low.

But during its decade-long run that started in 2001 up to its peak in 2011, *silver gained 1,080% - better than a tenfold gain.*

Given the extreme and unprecedented levels of stimulus, money-printing, and debt in the last few decades, I believe that we are still amid the silver bull market that started back in 2001.

We could well have another 5-6 years, or more, in front of us.

Silver Price 2001 - 2022

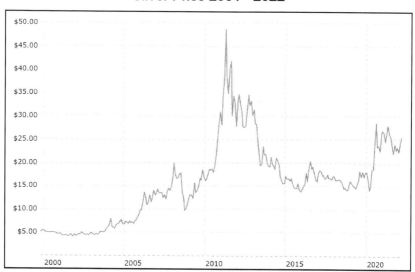

Source: macrotrends.net

I think silver's low of $13.70 in late 2015 was its cycle bottom. After a false start and a return to $14 in late 2018, silver's bull market action returned.

In 2020, silver's dramatic but short-lived selloff from $16 in early March to $12 and back to $16 came at the height of panic from the COVID-19 coronavirus pandemic. It took just one month to play out.

The fact that silver bottomed at $12, which was almost triple the $4.14 low in 2001, suggests to me that we are still in the same powerful multi-decade bull market. By June 2020, silver had already regained $18, and by August, it had soared to $29.

It seems the pandemic panic, or more accurately, government and central bank reactions to it, were the trigger that helped launch the next phase of the current silver bull market.

Key Takeaways

- The 1970s silver bull market generated a 3,740% gain.
- Between 2001 and 2011, silver gained 1,080%.
- We're likely in the 2nd half of a secular silver bull market, with much higher to go.

Chapter 28: Silver Outperforms Gold in Bull Markets

I detailed earlier for you why silver, like gold, is a precious and monetary metal.

However, as you know, one thing that clearly sets it apart from gold is its industrial uses. These account for about 50% of silver demand, whereas industrial applications only account for about 10% of gold's demand.

But the differences between silver and gold go well beyond that. There are numerous characteristics of silver and silver markets that can give you an edge over other investors if you understand them.

So, I'm dedicating this and the next few chapters to these peculiarities to help you become a better and more successful silver investor.

One interesting and helpful thing to know about silver is that it nearly consistently outperforms gold in bull markets. A term often used is that "silver is like gold on steroids," as it tends to generate even greater gains than gold, but often with a time lag.

The following table compares gold and silver returns over several bull markets.

Silver Outperforms Gold in Bull Markets

Bull Markets	GOLD	SILVER
1976-1980	717%	1,063%
1985-1987	75%	97%
2001-2008	289%	383%
2008-2011	164%	446%
2020 - April '21	22%	118%

Source: goldsilver.com

Of course, the standout here is the second half of the 1970s secular silver bull market, when from 1976 to 1980 silver dramatically outperformed gold. I expect a considerable outperformance this time around as well.

Here is another chart that plots the performance for some of these same silver bull markets.

Silver vs. Gold Performance
During Previous & Current Bull Markets

Source: Discovery Silver, Thomson Reuters, Silverseek.com

And here is yet another way to visualize silver against gold over the past 50 years.

We see the considerable outperformance of silver versus gold in terms of percentage gains, especially in 1980 and again in 2011.

Silver vs. Gold Prices 1970 - 2021

Source: macrotrends.net, silverstockinvestor.com

And as we can see on the far-right side of the chart, silver still has a lot of catching up to do versus gold to outperform again in this current bull market.

History has shown us that when gold is in a sharply rising bull market, silver ultimately outperforms it.

But why is that? Let's look at several reasons.

Key Takeaways

- Silver outperforms gold in bull markets, sometimes dramatically.
- This has happened multiples times since 1970.
- Silver still has a lot of catching up to do against gold.

Chapter 29: Silver – A Fraction of The Gold Market

This is one of my shortest chapters, but it makes a very big point.

The silver market is many times smaller than the gold market.

Using annual supply numbers, we can figure out how large both markets are on that basis. The total annual supply of gold is about 150 million ounces, which at $1,800/oz. is worth about $270 billion. The total annual silver supply is about 1 billion ounces, which at $27 is about $27 billion annually. So, the annual supply of gold is worth about ten times the annual supply of silver.

Therefore, it stands to reason that it takes much less buying or selling to push silver higher or lower. That also impacts silver price volatility, which is typically more pronounced both on the upside and the downside.

There are also fewer retail and institutional participants in the silver market than in the gold market. Remember, gold is held by many central banks, some investment banks and even some pension and sovereign wealth funds. Lower levels of liquidity tend to exacerbate price movements in the silver market.

One particularity of silver is that, while it usually outperforms gold in bull markets, that's often with a time lag. In the past, when silver investors became more certain that silver sentiment had turned negative and was expected to remain so for a while, they've sold their silver.

That's been less true for gold. But my research over the past few years has suggested that this may not apply to the same degree going forward.

In any case, with gold buyers being more diverse and more willing to simply hold, the gold bull market rises more gradually.

Key Takeaways

- The supply of gold is worth about 10 times the supply of silver.

- The much smaller silver market takes less buying or selling to move the price.

- Silver is more widely owned by individuals than large institutions.

Chapter 30: Spot Prices and Draining the Futures Market

If you're going to invest in silver, it's vital to understand how the silver price is determined, as well as the differences between "spot" and "physical" silver prices.

The "spot silver price" is the constantly fluctuating price that we see quoted throughout the day.

It is *not* the price you'll pay when buying physical silver.

Instead, the spot price is determined mostly by futures contracts, which are binding agreements to buy and sell silver for a particular price on a specific date. As explained by UK bullion dealer BullionByPost: "These contracts are a means for mines, mints, refiners, dealers, and buyers of silver to hedge the value of their metal against large fluctuations on the Silver Commodities Market. This brings some degree of stability to an otherwise volatile commodity market."

Technically, futures contracts are for the future delivery of large amounts of silver. However, nearly all trading in futures markets is to hedge risk or speculate. BullionByPost said: "Explained very simply: if a manufacturer needs one hundred ounces of silver to make their products, they can hedge risk over the production period by buying the physical metal, and at the same time buying future contract options on the same amount of silver. When they sell products, based on the silver price at that time, they can buy back the options and cover the risk."

I don't recommend trading in futures markets, especially for newer investors. They tend to be complex, expensive and can involve high levels of risk.

The London Bullion Market Association (LBMA) is a precious metals industry association. It sets standards for gold and silver bars (quality, size, etc.), with a list of refiners whose bars meet those standards.

When institutional asset managers, traders and investors look to buy or sell gold or silver on a larger scale, the banks they deal with usually buy or sell these bars. Typically, they remain within certain approved warehouses to maintain a chain of integrity. That provides assurance to all the participants that the bars held are the real deal.

However, since members are mostly major international banks, bullion dealers and refiners, some critics consider the LBMA as part of a cabal set out to manipulate prices. On a certain level, I can sympathize with those concerns.

Consider that one major task of the LBMA is to establish the silver price. Every weekday at 12 pm London time, a private auction amongst its ten member banks is held, whereby they determine the silver price for that day. That might sound archaic, and in my view, it is. I doubt that will last, especially when one considers how many silver-related contracts are set based on this price and the huge chasm between spot silver prices and physical silver prices at bullion dealers.

Fluctuations in the spot price are mostly determined by COMEX trading. COMEX is a division of the **Chicago Mercantile Exchange**, or CME. Spot silver prices are a composite of worldwide futures markets. But with COMEX as the world's largest futures and options market for trading metals, it's considered the most influential market for silver futures contracts.

As per bullion dealer APMEX, "Futures contracts for Silver on the COMEX represent the projected price of 5,000 ounces of Silver on a hypothetical future delivery date. However, most futures contracts are never settled in Physical Silver, just cash. Hundreds of ounces of 'on-paper' Silver are traded on the

COMEX for every single ounce of Physical Silver that is ultimately delivered in the real world."

Although the spot silver price is the one most discussed and quoted, physical silver prices are higher - often considerably higher. I will explain exactly why in **Chapter 41 - Physical Silver**. For now, consider that the gap between spot and physical prices is typically large. Many believe there is outright manipulation of silver markets, especially given their smaller size.

An August 2020 report by Macquarie determined the leverage ratios of derivatives to physical markets for various exchange-traded commodities. In the case of gold, that ratio was 74. And nickel was in second place with a ratio of 86. Silver was by far the leader, with a derivative to physical metal ratio of 193. This is one big reason silver prices can be volatile.

In this same vein, there have been interesting developments recently involving the futures markets and physical silver.

In a late 2021 interview with *Quoth the Raven*, Andy Shectman, president and owner of **Miles Franklin Precious Metals**, described recent happenings in the silver market.

> *"The physical demand filters down from the top. Over 300 million ounces of silver were removed from the COMEX market in 2020 by some of the most sophisticated and well-heeled investors in the world. Settlements on the COMEX are usually mostly in dollars. The COMEX was not set up to be a source of physical delivery. This is no small development. In years past, this amount would represent roughly a decade's worth of silver deliveries. In addition, COMEX deliveries in 2021 are now on pace to better the*

*2020's delivery numbers. When all of this is
added to record global retail physical demand in
coins and bars - physical demand at some point
and probably sooner rather than later, will
completely overwhelm supply."*

Of course, it's impossible to know whether futures markets will continue being used to access physical silver. If they are, this will remain an additional drain on supply that has recently become much more substantial.

In my view, the significant difference between spot and physical prices cannot be sustained. As physical prices remain considerably higher, I expect that spot prices will rise over time to catch up to physical prices.

Key Takeaways

- Spot silver prices are not the same as physical silver prices.
- Silver futures contracts are used by miners, traders, and large institutions to hedge or speculate.
- Spot silver will likely rise considerably to reflect much higher physical silver prices.

Chapter 31: Silver is a FOMO Target

In case you're not familiar with it, FOMO is an acronym for "Fear of Missing Out." In short, it's investor emotion - greed - in its most visceral form.

And it's very real.

In this chapter. I'm going to show you how FOMO influences silver prices in a very real way, too.

And I'll show you how to use the emotions of others to your advantage.

FOMO is the anxiety of not being included in something enjoyable, interesting, or rewarding. Social media plays a big role, as users are continually connected with what others are doing. There's even an element of regret - people worry they will "miss out" on a social event or even a profitable investment.

In Chapter 38, you'll see how a social media storm in early 2021 caused silver prices to explode nearly 20% higher in just days. That event also launched the Reddit online discussion forum, *Wall Street Silver*, that grew within a year to over 180,000 members. Many of them are young silver enthusiasts, now part of a new and growing community.

Fear is a very powerful motivator, and FOMO simply multiplies its effects. It's often been said of precious metals that higher prices beget even higher prices. I believe this is FOMO working at its best.

In nearly every other market, when prices rise, demand falls off. Rising prices usually cause buyers to seek cheaper substitutes or alternatives. Also, when things function normally in a supply/demand market, supply will rise to meet higher demand, causing prices to fall back or plateau.

Silver and gold turn this premise on its head. Remember, they're not regular commodities - they're chaos hedges. These metals go through strong rallies that often feed on themselves as observers become participants, and new buying leads to still more buying.

In January 2010, at the World Economic Forum, the famous hedge fund manager George Soros gave an interview. He said, "When interest rates are low, we have conditions for asset bubbles to develop, and they are developing now. The ultimate asset bubble is gold."

Soros's timing was impeccable. Between January 2010 and September 2011, gold went from $1,100 to a then all-time high of $1,920 per ounce. It was a spectacular 18-month run, and it was clear and outright FOMO.

We saw in **Chapter 28** that silver has historically outperformed gold in bull markets. As a gold bull market matures, more investors become increasingly aware of the metal's performance as its gains are widely reported. That leads investors to start paying more attention and eventually deciding they want a "piece of the gold bull market action."

However, this usually happens once the gold bull market has already become quite mature. Bull markets are famous for drawing in the most participants during later phases. Once new prospective gold investors realize how expensive an ounce of gold is, they turn to its cheaper alternative: silver. They see silver as giving them much more "bang for their buck." This is a parallel to buyers seeking cheaper substitutes or alternatives, as I mentioned earlier.

A wave of silver buying hits as investors want a piece of the rising precious metals bull market. So, they rapidly "bid up" the silver price, causing its gains to outpace those of gold. I believe this is one of the major reasons silver outperforms gold in bull

184

markets.

Still, as investors, we need to stay open to the possibility that things may not play out the same way every time.

Thanks to the COVID-19 pandemic and widespread government stimulus reaction, the silver market has piqued the interest of a broader group of investors. Several factors, including a push for green energy and social media campaigns encouraging silver buying, have injected new-and-younger buyers into the silver market.

I'll show you more about this powerful shift a bit later in the book. For now, you just need to understand that they'll cause prices to surge faster than they have in past silver rallies.

Key Takeaways

- Silver is a perfect target for FOMO - the "Fear of Missing Out."
- As precious metals markets mature, investors move from gold to silver.
- Silver may start outperforming gold earlier in this bull market thanks to favorable drivers.

Chapter 32: Understanding the Gold/Silver Ratio

Tracking the relationship between silver and gold prices can be a lucrative way to invest in silver.

The gold/silver ratio is a simple tool that gives investors some sense of whether silver is costly, cheap, or priced fairly relative to gold. It's basically the number of silver ounces required to buy one gold ounce, calculated by dividing the gold price by the silver price.

Since 1975, the gold/silver ratio has averaged about 55-60, meaning it has taken about 55-60 silver ounces to buy one gold ounce.

There are a few important takeaways from the following multi-decade chart.

Gold/Silver Ratio 1975 - 2021

Source: goldprice.org, silverstockinvestor.com

Firstly, the ratio hit an ultimate low near 15 when silver peaked at $50 in 1980. It hit another low near 30 when silver topped at

$49 again in 2011.

Secondly, we see that the ratio often tends to peak near 80. This suggests that when it takes 80 or more ounces of silver to buy one ounce of gold, silver has become too cheap relative to gold. Then ratio tends to reverse, and the silver price starts to outperform the gold price.

Keep in mind this does not automatically mean the silver price will rise faster than the gold price. It can also mean that the silver price will fall more slowly than the gold price, and so it outperforms gold despite falling. It's also possible for the silver price to rise while the gold price falls, though this rarely happens for extended periods, as silver typically will trend in the same direction as gold.

Thirdly, note that since the ratio bottomed in 2011, it rose quite steadily, then quickly soared to an all-time high at the peak of the COVID-19 pandemic panic in March 2020, reaching an eye-watering 125. From there, the ratio fell back very quickly to 70, with silver dramatically outperforming gold.

I believe that's a strong indication silver has entered what I call the acceleration phase. In my view, silver is likely to continue outperforming gold in this bull market. Where will the ratio finally bottom? I'll give you my prediction shortly.

When the ratio is falling from a high level - especially from above 80 - it often means that both gold and silver are in a bull market. And with silver outpacing gold, you need to pay careful attention.

Key Takeaways

- The Gold/Silver ratio tells us how many ounces of silver it takes to buy an ounce of gold.
- When the ratio peaks at or above 80 and starts to fall, it usually indicates a good time to buy silver.

- The Gold/Silver ratio bottomed at 15 in 1980, and at 30 in 2011.

Chapter 33: Silver Is Volatile

Don't let silver's volatility scare you away. Instead, make it work for you.

For now, understand that volatility is one of silver's hallmarks which, for some, is part of its appeal. In fact, it's an opportunity. In **Chapter 53 - The Five Secrets for Managing Risk**, I'll show you simple ways you can lessen risk, including from volatility.

Naturally, it's a double-edged sword. But knowing volatility exists, and expecting it, will make it easier to deal with. Harnessing that volatility makes it work to your advantage. And that can be very rewarding.

Between 2002 and 2006, silver dropped 10% or more four separate times.

Notable Silver Price Corrections 2002 - 2006

Source: silverstockinvestor.com

Then, between 2006 and 2011, shorter but sometimes deep corrections followed, with silver dropping 13% or more three times.

Notable Silver Price Corrections 2006 - 2011

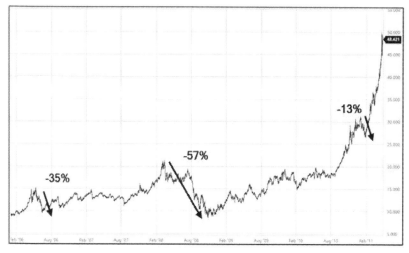

Source: silverstockinvestor.com

From 2001 until its peak in 2011, silver gave back 20% or more four times. But the real takeaway is that anyone who held on from the beginning enjoyed an astounding 1,080% gain.

The key is knowing whether silver is still in a bull market. That way, you are more willing to sit through corrections, even deeper ones, without selling. But this doesn't mean you just sit on your hands and do nothing.

Some investors choose to lighten their exposure to silver by perhaps selling some or selling certain silver investments. This is all fine and depends on personal risk tolerance. But having and holding a core position makes sense to maintain ongoing exposure.

Key Takeaways

- Silver is volatile. With proper risk management, that can work in your favour.

- Understanding and expecting silver volatility makes it easier to manage.

- Silver volatility can be harnessed to increase investments or take profits.

Chapter 34: Major Silver Spikes

We know from history that once silver awakens from its slumber, it often soars.

The metal goes through price spikes that can be enormous but often short-lived.

The following chart shows all the major silver spikes from 1973 to 2020.

Size and Duration of Major Silver Price Spikes 1973 - 2020

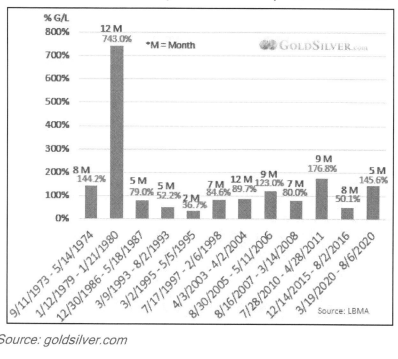

Source: goldsilver.com

This table averages all the spikes detailed above.

Average Gain, Duration and Time Between Silver Spikes

Silver Spikes	
GOLDSILVER.com	
Average Gain	150.4%
Average Duration	7.4 mos
Average Time Between Spikes	3 yrs, 6 mos

Source: goldsilver.com

These spikes come fast and furious. That doesn't mean that the price rises dramatically and gives back all its gains, though sometimes that can happen. Other times, the price moves in a sideways range after rallying.

For example, silver dropped to $12 in March 2020, then by early August, it had spiked to near $30. That was a 145% gain in just five months. After that huge move, the silver price "digested" those gains, moving in a trading range between $22 and $29 for over 20 months. It was building a new base as it prepared to run higher.

Silver Price Chart March 2017 - 2022

Source: silverprice.org, silverstockinvestor.com

Here's what you need to remember.

First, to benefit from these spikes, you need to be invested. Second, they can make for excellent opportunities to lock in profits and reduce risk when they arrive. That allows you to raise capital and wait for the next inflection point.

On the other hand, when sentiment weighs heavily against silver, that can signal that it's time to take advantage of bargains and buy oversold silver and silver stocks.

Key Takeaways

- Silver is known for going through huge price spikes.
- Although the spikes tend to be short-lived, the price will often remain at a new higher level afterwards.
- You need to be invested to benefit and use spikes to take profits.

Chapter 35: Silver Seasonality

Seasonality is a phenomenon in the investment and trading markets. As you'll see, it clearly affects silver prices. And you can turn it to your advantage.

Keep in mind; other factors will often have more influence, especially on individual stocks. But don't ignore the power of seasonality on resource prices themselves.

If we can glean patterns from how silver behaves based on the time of year, we can use that to our benefit. Now, this is like many other indicators. It exists because observations over long periods show there are clear trends.

However, in any given year, the seasonal pattern may not repeat to the same degree as it does on average. Sometimes, in a particular year, the trend acts very differently. Consider too that the seasonal trend for silver will also vary depending on whether silver is in a bear market, is trading mostly sideways, or is in a bull market.

So, what drives seasonality? Well, it's usually a combination of things.

As you might expect, silver tends to follow gold's lead. So, it's no surprise that silver seasonality is *like* gold. Gold typically enjoys strength in the fall. Indians are big gold buyers, and they buy with excess cash following their harvest season. Hindus will often wait to make larger gold purchases for their fall festivals of Dhanteras and Diwali.

In the West, that's followed by the year-end Christmas/New Year holiday season and then Valentine's Day in February. Like Indians, the Chinese also have a strong affinity for gold. So, with the Chinese Lunar New Year falling around late January/early February, there's plenty of gold buying taking place early in the year.

These are just a few examples of what causes seasonality for gold and, to a fair extent, also silver.

Let's look at a seasonal chart for silver prices.

Silver Seasonality 1975 - 2021

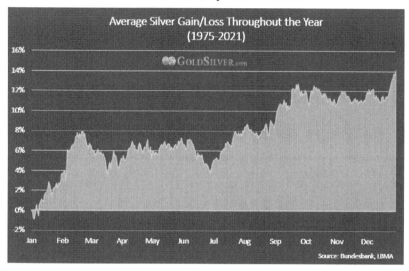

Source: goldsilver.com

As you can see, silver's strongest period starts in the fall and, on average, runs higher from September through February. It can have early spring weakness, followed by renewed strength, then more weakness mid-summer, before rising again.

So, on this basis, the best times of year to buy silver tend to be July, September, and December.

Another factor that weighs on silver in the summer is traders. Silver futures prices highly influence the silver spot price and, like many of us, traders take time off during the summer months in the northern hemisphere. As a result, many traders will close out positions until they return to work. This triggers additional selling that's less present most of the rest of the year.

And that leads to a phenomenon known as the summer doldrums. That's when precious metals and their miners face the weakest period of the year. While individual silver stocks are more dependent on company news, the silver price certainly amplifies their movements. Junior silver stocks are somewhat more likely to move based on good or bad news relating to discovery, a joint venture, an asset sale or purchase, or a merger or acquisition.

Also, with or without a resource, junior silver stocks are more reliant than the rest of the sector on drill results. Depending on where their projects are located, some can be drilled year-round, while others can't. Typically, the farther north they are located, the more difficult or impossible it is to access and drill in the winter or even spring months. This can include locations such as some northern U.S. states or portions of some Canadian provinces and territories. It can also be an issue in places like Scandinavia or Northern Europe.

So limited access means that, for those projects, exploration and drilling may only begin in May or June. A few months may have passed when the first set of drill holes is complete, with lab results back and interpreted. Then the first news releases from an exploration campaign only arrive in July or August, leading to quietness or market weakness in the earlier part of the summer.

Consider too that silver stocks, like silver itself, are also affected by traders, retail investors and asset managers who take time away from their computer screens. This leads to lower trading volumes as well as lower share prices as participants' interest temporarily wanes.

But these periods of consolidation, when the silver price retreats or moves sideways, are often a great time to buy. Significant price bottoms are established during July and August. The best investors often wait for these opportunities to deploy capital, allowing them to pick up quality silver stocks on the cheap.

One other period of weakness to mention, especially in Canada and the U.S., is tax-loss selling season, which typically runs the last few weeks of December. Investors will sell their losing positions to crystallize losses, allowing them to offset capital gains earned during that calendar year. They do this as part of tax planning to minimize taxes payable. This period can also make for an excellent opportunity for shrewd investors to buy silver stocks on temporary weakness.

Key Takeaways

- History shows that silver prices fluctuate somewhat predictably based on seasonal trends.
- The summer is quiet as traders and investors take vacation, and year-end brings weakness from tax-loss selling.
- Astute silver investors use these periods of weakness and strength to their advantage.

Chapter 36: Silver is Historically Cheap

We've all heard the investing maxim "buy low, sell high."

And with good reason: If there's one sure-fire way to increase your potential gains while also lowering risk, it's to buy a stock, bond, commodity, or other asset when it's cheap.

And no matter how you look at it, silver is exceedingly cheap...for now.

As I like to say, there's nothing like zooming out to get a wider perspective. It's often a reflex to just focus on daily, monthly, or even yearly data for a particular asset to understand what might come next. But long-term charts offer a very different viewpoint.

This chart shows the silver price over the last 50 years.

Silver Price 1971 - 2021

Source: silverprice.org

We can clearly see that, in that time frame, silver has twice flirted with the $50 level, both in 1980 and 2011. And despite over 40 years having passed since silver's first peak at $50 in 1980, silver is still about 50% below that all-time nominal high. It's amazing to think that, after so long and so much fiat money printing, silver is still so inexpensive.

Let's now look at silver adjusted for inflation. In my view, this is more realistic, because prices for practically everything rise over time in conjunction with input costs. It's a natural progression.

Inflation-Adjusted Silver Price 1971 - 2021

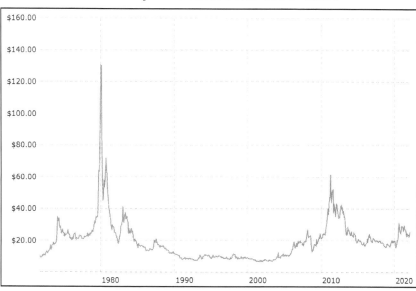

Source: macrotrends.net

As you can see, the $125 peak shown in this chart is nearly five times the current (roughly $25) price of silver. Even the 2011 $50 peak, adjusted for inflation, is $60 today, and that's still 2.4 times higher than the current price of silver.

The $125 peak depicted above chart is likely based on an average monthly price - and should probably be closer to $170 to account for silver's $50 peak. Using the U.S. Bureau of Labor Statistics' own CPI Inflation Calculator, $50 in January 1980 equates to $174 today.

While that might sound high, consider this: from its 1971 low of $1.31 to its 1980 high of $50, silver generated a massive return of 3,740%. When the bull market started in 2001, silver hit a low of $4.14. If we calculate a return of that same magnitude (37.4 times), that takes us to a peak of $155.

A look at the Dow/silver ratio suggests that silver is especially cheap in comparison to the broad stock market. It also suggests that the broader markets may be quite expensive.

Dow/Silver Ratio 1970 - 2022

Source: macrotrends.net, silverstockinvestor.com

To obtain this ratio, we divide the Dow Jones Industrial Average Index by the silver price.

The Dow/silver ratio bottomed at 24.5 in 1980 when silver peaked at $50. If we apply that to today, we get an astounding number. At a ratio of 24.5, with the Dow at 35,000, silver would be priced at...$1,429 per ounce!

Now, I'm not suggesting that silver is going to anywhere near $1,400. But, hey, weirder things have happened. Besides, the Dow could drop - perhaps precipitously - and I think it likely will. Let's say the Dow falls 50% to 17,500. That would still imply a silver price of $715 – a long way from today's $25.

This next chart is perhaps a little bit quirky, but it's certainly interesting. Essentially, it compares the price of silver to the average home price in the U.S. market.

Silver/Average U.S. Home Price Ratio 1975 - 2021

Source: goldsilver.com

Silver was at its cheapest over the past 50 years versus real estate back in 2000-2004. Back then, it took as much as 55,000 ounces of silver to buy the typical American home. That has changed, with silver prices having risen considerably.

In late-2021, the average U.S. home sales price was $478,000, while an ounce of silver cost $23. The ratio tells us that it takes about 21,000 silver ounces to buy the average U.S. home.

In 2011 when silver peaked near $49, it took just 5,500 ounces. And back in 1980, at silver's secular bull high of $50, it took just 1,464 silver ounces. This, too, suggests silver is still inexpensive.

But this next table is probably the most telling. It gives us the prices of several base and precious metals at their 1980 highs compared to their levels in November 2021.

Precious and Base Metals Prices 1980 Vs. 2021

Silver Is the Only Metal Priced Below 1980 High			
	1980 High	Nov. 26, 2021	Change
Copper	$1	$4.46	225.5%
Lead	$1,166	$2,330	99.8%
Nickel	$6,979	$21,063	201.8%
Zinc	$867	$3,431	295.7%
Tin	$17,461	$40,950	134.5%
Iron Ore	$12	$94	686.1%
Platinum	$752	$951	26.5%
Palladium	$350	$1,688	382.3%
Rhodium	$833	$12,500	1,400.6%
Gold	$850	$1,785	110.0%
Silver	$50	$23.09	-53.8%
GOLDSILVER.com	Sources: LBMA, macrotrends.net, businessinsider.com		

Source: goldsilver.com

It's simply astounding to see that most metals have doubled or tripled, while some are up 6x and even 14x.

Silver is the clear standout. In fact, it's the only one that is below its 1980 high. And not just somewhat below. At today's price around $25, silver is still 50% below its 1980 peak. That's just senseless. If you calculate silver's drop from the $50 peak adjusted for inflation at $174, silver is currently down by 85%.

As part of my ongoing research, I follow a lot of assets. I honestly can't think of one easily investable sector as cheap as silver is today. And that makes silver and silver stocks very exciting as we look forward.

Key Takeaways

- Silver is exceptionally cheap based on several indicators.

- Silver is 50% below its 1980 all-time high, and 85% below that inflation-adjusted high.

- Compared to stocks, real estate and all other major metals, silver is still a bargain.

Chapter 37: Silver is Sticky Money

In my experience, people who buy silver are very reluctant to sell it.

And that has important investment implications.

That's especially true for physical silver and, to some extent, silver investments like Exchange Traded Funds (ETFs), also known as Exchange Traded Products (ETPs). These investments are like shares traded on a stock exchange and represent partial ownership of silver.

Each silver ETF is structured somewhat differently, but all essentially aim to track silver price movements, with most offering a claim on silver. I will delve into silver ETFs in more detail in a later chapter. In the last several years, silver ETFs have become quite popular, with the first having been launched in 2006. One big reason is that investors can gain exposure to silver with just a few clicks on their computer and hold that investment in their brokerage accounts.

While examining the following chart of silver ETP holdings overlayed with the silver price, I noticed a particular relationship between these in recent years. I dubbed it: "Silver is Sticky Money."

As this chart shows across several years, even when the silver price experienced significant drops, total silver holdings by ETPs tended to only drop minimally, stay flat, or even increase. I've pointed out some of those instances with arrows.

Global Silver ETP Holdings vs. Silver Price 2008 - March 2021

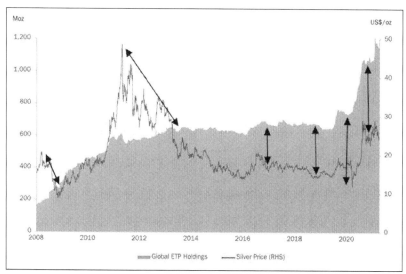

Source: lbma.org, silverstockinvestor.com

What this suggests is that once most investors in silver ETPs have bought, they typically hang on.

It's interesting that investor interest in silver picked up substantially after nearly four years of mainly stable holdings. In late 2019 we saw a surge in silver ETP holdings, then a move sideways until early 2020. That's when the COVID-19 pandemic panic hit, and silver prices were temporarily hammered down to $12 per ounce. But notice that silver ETP holdings hardly budged at that point, then quickly began climbing along with the silver price through the rest of 2020.

In fact, silver price action from the pandemic panic lows of March 2020 through to early 2021 and beyond was nothing short of breathtaking. Silver ETP buying was through the roof. According to the Silver Institute's World Silver Survey 2021, silver ETPs acquired a net 331 million ounces, up 298% over 2019's already high 83 million ounces. For a little perspective, 331 million ounces represents about 34% of the entire silver supply for 2020. What's more, by end-2021, silver ETPs alone had accumulated total holdings of 1.13 billion ounces, which is more than an entire year's supply.

In my view silver demand from ETPs will continue to be strong, especially as this bull market progresses. And that should help keep a solid, rising floor under silver prices.

Key Takeaways

- Silver buyers tend to hold onto it for a very long time, so "Silver is Sticky Money."

- Silver ETF holdings tend to remain stable even when silver prices drop.

- Silver ETF holdings have soared, with total inventories over 1 billion ounces, more than a whole year's supply of silver.

Chapter 38: Silver Squeeze 2.0

After the famous silver squeeze by the Hunt Brothers (detailed in Chapter 6), it was a long time before silver would again hit the headlines in a big way.

That finally happened in early 2021, when an intriguing new event triggered "Silver Squeeze 2.0."

And it came to us courtesy of WallStreetBets (WSB), an online discussion subgroup on the Reddit website, a forum where users discuss the stocks they buy and sell. In early 2021, group members targeted GameStop Corp. (NYSE: GME), the biggest computer-game retailer - because they realized hedge funds were heavily shorting the company's shares.

When investors short a stock, they're essentially borrowing the company's shares, selling them at the current trading price to reap the proceeds, betting they can buy them back (and return them) later at a much lower price - and pocketing the difference for a profit.

WSB suggested participants buy GameStop shares to push the price higher. Since group members felt the "hedgies" were intentionally suppressing GameStop's share price, they decided to create a "short squeeze" that would hammer the institutional speculators and cause them to lose money. WSB argued that if enough investors bought GameStop shares, pushing its price higher, the hedge funds would be forced to cover their short positions by buying the stock, thereby driving the price even higher.

The "short squeeze" strategy was wildly successful - igniting a run that caused GameStop shares to zoom from under $20 in mid-January to a peak at $483 - in a mere week and a half. It worked so well, in fact, that hedge fund Melvin Capital (which had a hefty short position) required an emergency $2.8 billion

208

bailout. While such a lofty price wasn't sustainable, even six months later GameStop shares were still trading at $185.

After the GameStop affair, a WSB post essentially encouraged its members to buy the silver focused SLV ETF to help trigger a squeeze on the short position in silver futures. Since SLV is supposed to buy physical silver to support new buying of its shares, the idea was that this ETF would do so much buying it would "squeeze out" the short position in silver futures.

Reddit's WSB subreddit was titled: "The biggest short squeeze in the world $SLV Silver $25 to $1000." Here's a portion of that post from Jan. 28, 2021:

Post From WSB, Jan. 28, 2021

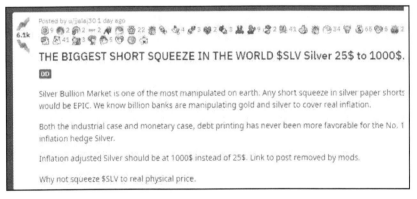

Source: reddit.com

By all accounts, followers bought SLV *en masse*, and the spot silver price blasted higher from $25 to $29.50 within just three trading days, along with the ETF. Silver normally follows gold higher, yet this happened while the gold price remained flat. I tracked this all in real-time on my computer screen as *the average silver stock was up about 30% to 40% in only three trading days. Share volumes were up 6-7 times, and SLV saw nine times its normal daily volume.*

All this action forced the managers of the SLV ETF to add 37 million shares to the trust in one day and buy an estimated 1,150 metric tonnes of silver. In essence, these message boards were introducing many people to silver investing for the first time. Investment banks have been "net short" silver futures for years (if not decades), happy to see low silver prices as they help mask true inflation. So WSB followers tried to force those "shorts" into the market to buy physical silver.

Spot silver prices gradually fell back to around $25 within about one month as buying pressure waned. The rapid and sizeable gains in silver stocks also dissipated. But it's important to note that the spot price for silver does not include premiums. It's simply an "official" price for silver which is used to set conditions for contracts, for example.

Since the COVID-19 pandemic hit in March 2020, bullion dealers were already short on inventory, as people were actively buying plenty of silver and gold coins and bars. That continued all through 2020 and into 2021. But when this silver squeeze hit, it ignited the demand for physical silver to another level overnight.

During the weekend of Jan. 30-31, 2021, bullion dealers were swamped, and some were quite literally overwhelmed. Many had never in their decades of experience witnessed such a rapid tsunami of demand. Their already meagre inventories were drained within a couple of days. Some were fielding so many phone calls and online purchases over that weekend, their computer systems crashed. Others deliberately limited buying or closed temporarily because their inventories were nonexistent. Interestingly, many said orders were on the smaller side, indicating that individual retail customers made up the bulk of buyers.

Premiums on silver coins and bars, which had already been at double normal levels, rose to triple normal levels. That took premiums to 50% above the spot price of silver. And this persisted for many months afterwards as buying pressure stayed elevated. Inventories remained sparse, with many of the most popular coins out of stock for months on end, and delivery delays going from 2-3 days to 2-3 weeks.

This highlights just how small the silver market is and how it reacts to such drivers. But since this wasn't a fundamental trigger, like a mine supply shortage, I didn't expect this impulse buying to lead to a sustained move higher in silver prices. That's what I told my subscribers, and that's how it played out.

However, this event did make a lot of younger people, an entire new generation in fact, aware of silver, precious metals, and real money for the first time. And that may well be a permanent shift in their mindset. As I mentioned in Chapter 31, within just one year, the Wall Street Silver subreddit online discussion forum reached an impressive 180,000 members, all keen on actively following silver markets. It even spurred the Wall Street Silver YouTube channel with 45,000 subscribers, and the Wall Street Silver Twitter account with nearly 100,000 followers.

For silver investors, this is the biggest takeaway from the entire event. And it could fundamentally change the nature of this silver bull market going forward.

Key Takeaways

- In early 2021 silver experienced a social media induced squeeze, causing silver and silver stocks to soar, and introduced silver investing to a new generation of investors.
- Silver ETFs and silver stocks saw massive buying.
- Bullion dealers were overwhelmed by silver orders, causing premiums to soar.

Chapter 39: Fallout from Silver Squeeze 2.0

In addition to setting the London silver price (see Chapter 30), the London Bullion Market Association (LBMA) also tracks the physical silver inventories it holds for several ETFs, including SLV (the largest silver ETF). The LBMA keeps accounts of who owns how much of the metal.

But with silver being a non-producing asset with a holding cost (warehousing, insurance, etc.), some large silver holders choose to lease out their silver to earn interest. That causes concern, because some of the parties the silver is leased to also claim control of that silver. At that point, you have two claims on the very same silver, which many people naturally find troubling.

In April 2021, just over two months after the WSB call to squeeze the silver shorts, the LMBA produced its *Silver Investment 2021: Report*. This report was prepared, at least in part, using demand figures from the Metals Focus Five-Year Silver Forecast.

The LMBA report highlighted how the previous 12-18 months had witnessed astounding developments in the silver market, with a massive surge in investment activity. It pointed out how total demand and net managed money positioning had risen about 20% to roughly $10 billion, the second-highest level Metals Focus had recorded in the past decade.

What's most notable in the report, given the LMBA's role in the market, is the statement: "Early 2021 saw an unprecedented 110Moz added in just three days. Although some liquidations emerged, there were concerns that London would run out of silver if ETP demand remained at a high level."

That's not the sort of admission you'd expect to hear from the

LBMA. They also acknowledged that the 331 million ounces that flowed into ETFs in 2020 were well beyond anything in the previous decade. In fact, according to the Silver Institute's World Silver Survey 2021, it was almost four times the prior year's high, which was 83 million ounces in 2019.

Referring to the silver surge in late January/early February, the LBMA report points out:

"Global ETP holdings hit a record high of 1,207Moz. on Feb. 2, 2021. As impressive as this may appear, it does not tell the whole story. As the social media frenzy gathered pace in late January, demand for coins, bars and ETPs all jumped. For the latter, global holdings surged by 119Moz in just three days. This was concentrated in the iShares fund, where holdings rose by 110Moz. Given that most of this metal was allocated in London, fears emerged as to whether there was enough silver should demand continue at this pace. At end-February 2021, 765Moz was allocated in London against ETPs, leaving 360Moz of potentially available metal. This suggests that had demand in iShares continued at the frenetic rate of late-January/early February it would only have been a matter of weeks before London's existing stock was used up. While it would have been surprising to see ETP demand maintain this pace of buying, the concerns were still very real. This reflects both the time required for a

refinery to convert non-Good Delivery (GDL) material into 1,000oz bars approved by LBMA as Good Delivery and then delivery of this by sea freight into London.

Another way to view this is to look at combined COMEX/LBMA holdings, which at end February were 1,518Moz. ETPs vaulted in these locations stood at 880Moz, which meant that 42%, or 638Moz, was in theory immediately available to meet new silver ETP demand. However, it is not that straightforward. This does not take into account any challenges in moving metal between London vaults, nor any hurdles in being able to ramp-up ETP allocations on COMEX, versus London. It does suggest that the pool of available metal should be sufficient, for the foreseeable future at least, to meet new ETP demand. This also pre-supposes there is no repeat of the social media frenzy. Should this occur, higher prices would almost certainly be triggered, which would be met by heavy selling."

So, the LBMA acknowledges there were concerns about meeting demand during the silver squeeze. It further admits that a new surge in demand could cause a shortage, with vaulted silver supply unable to meet requirements, leading to a possible new spike in silver prices. We also know that within days of the silver squeeze, the iShares Silver Trust prospectus was changed, with the following added:

"The demand for silver may temporarily exceed

available supply that is acceptable for delivery to the Trust, which may adversely affect an investment in the Shares.

To the extent that demand for silver exceeds the available supply at that time, Authorized Participants may not be able to readily acquire sufficient amounts of silver necessary for the creation of a Basket.

Baskets may be created only by Authorized Participants and are only issued in exchange for an amount of silver determined by the Trustee that meets the specifications described below under 'Description of the Shares and the Trust Agreement– Deposit of Silver; Issuance of Baskets' on each day that NYSE Arca is open for regular trading. Market speculation in silver could result in increased requests for the issuance of Baskets.

It is possible that Authorized Participants may be unable to acquire sufficient silver that is acceptable for delivery to the Trust for the issuance of new Baskets due to a limited then available supply coupled with a surge in demand for the Shares.

In such circumstances, the Trust may suspend or restrict the issuance of Baskets. Such occurrence may lead to further volatility in Share price and deviations, which may be significant,

*in the market price of the Shares relative to the
NAV.*"

But what transpired after that was truly bizarre and quite
concerning. In April 2021, the LBMA published its monthly vault
data, indicating that London vaulted silver bars were up 11%
from 1.125 billion ounces to almost 1.25 billion ounces at the
end of March, a 124-million-ounce increase, setting a record.

But then, on May 10, the LBMA released a statement saying:

"A data submission error led to the publication of an incorrect
aggregate figure for the total silver held in London vaults in
March. The corrected figure is 1,143,194 Troy ounces ('00s)."

Apparently, one of the six vault operators had submitted
incorrect data. A monthly increase of 11% is nearly four times
the largest monthly increase previously recorded. And that
should have caused the LBMA to re-examine the data before
publishing. This is a major embarrassment and blemish on the
LBMA and frankly, in my opinion, not excusable for such an
institution.

Consider that the approximate 110 million silver ounces that
were overstated for March is very close to the quantity that SLV
had to acquire in just a few days as the silver squeeze caused
massive SLV buying. This casts doubt on whether that silver
ever did move from a vault operator into SLV's inventory.
Consider too those 110 million silver ounces, in 1,000-ounce
bars, are equal to 110,000 bars. That's about 3,700 pallets, each
with 30 bars, that had to be moved to SLV's designated vault...all
within about three days. And this was then followed by the SLV's
prospectus changes.

There seem to be a lot of odd coincidences and events that
happened to these various related parties over just a few
months' time. And there are a lot of unanswered questions

surrounding these events. Suffice it to say that one significant impact of the silver squeeze seems to have been to cast doubt on the inner workings of some of the largest institutions that deal with physical silver. And that's sure to encourage proponents of the silver squeeze to maintain their efforts.

So, now that you've read all about the quirks of silver, let's talk about where silver is headed. Because ultimately, that's what matters.

If you can really understand and appreciate how high silver is likely to go, then you'll better grasp its potential to help you achieve your goals of financial security and independence.

Key Takeaways

- Following the 2021 silver squeeze, the LBMA admitted there were concerns at the time of running out of silver.
- A new silver squeeze could trigger another spike in silver prices.
- Serious doubts were raised about SLV silver inventories reflecting outstanding shares.

Chapter 40: $300 Silver –
How We Get There

"For the record, I will state there will be another, more frenzied scramble which will carry silver prices to highs that will repair all the excess paper money creation, price suppression, supply deficit, and bearish sentiment of the past two decades. This will become known as the Great Silver Crisis."

DAVID MORGAN, C. 2002

It's tough to make predictions.

Still, silver is amid its biggest bull market in a generation.

That's why I'm predicting that silver will reach $300 an ounce over the next few years.

It's a big number, I know. You might even think that it's crazy (or that I am).

But if there's "madness" at work here, there's also a "method" that backs it.

Indeed, this isn't a number I've pulled out of thin air. Neither is it a prediction I've made lightly.

It's not an attempt at sensationalism.

This is an estimate relating to the gold price and inflation, and it's based on how gold and silver have performed in previous bull markets.

In fact, I'm going to show you several ways I arrive at my

estimate of $300.

But with gold so closely watched, let's first see where it's going.

Why Gold is Headed to $5,000 - $10,000 an ounce

We need to consider gold because it has so much influence on silver, especially during a bull market. I believe gold will ultimately peak at $5,000 per ounce. In fact, I've been saying publicly - going all the way back to 2010 - that gold will reach that level.

And truth be told, while I've adhered to my $5,000-an-ounce "call" on gold, I won't be stunned in the least if the "yellow metal" ultimately traverses the $10,000 plateau.

Several high-profile/well-known analysts have similar targets, and they've been carefully researched.

Back in 2009, Shayne McGuire was head of research and a portfolio manager at the Teacher Retirement System of Texas. He launched and managed the Trust's Gold Fund, the first dedicated precious metals fund in the U.S. pension system.

The next year, he published his book, *Hard Money: Taking Gold to a Higher Investment Level* and used a chapter on gold supply and demand to support his forecast that gold could soar to $10,000 an ounce. And that was back in 2010.

Perhaps one of the most notable gold forecasts comes from Scott Minerd. Thanks to Minerd's pedigree, multiple roles, and connections, it would be easy to label him as a member of the "establishment." Minerd is the chairman of Guggenheim Investments and global chief investment officer of Guggenheim Partners. He is also a member of the Federal Reserve Bank of New York's Investor Advisory Committee on Financial Markets, an advisor to the Organization for Economic Cooperation and Development (OECD), and a contributing member to the World

Economic Forum. You don't expect cautious and conservative institutions like these to call for big spikes in gold and silver prices.

And yet, in May 2021, Minerd told CNBC that his top price target for gold was $5,000 to $10,000, and that "this ultimately is in the cards. Silver traditionally lags. It is the poor man's gold, and it's the one that will have the largest move on a percentage basis. It is the high beta version of gold." He also said gold would enter an "exponential phase."

In January 2020, at the World Economic Forum's annual meeting in Davos, Switzerland, Minerd told *Bloomberg Surveillance* that his No. 1 conviction trade was silver. When asked why not gold, he said that silver was still 65% below its prior peak, whereas gold was getting very close to its previous peak. When asked if silver could go exponential, Miner said he thought there was a high probability of that happening.

My favourite, detailed prediction of a gold price peak comes from James G. Rickards. He is an American lawyer, economist, and investment banker with 40 years of capital markets experience on Wall Street. He was the principal negotiator for the rescue of Long-Term Capital Management L.P. (LTCM) by the U.S Federal Reserve in 1998. His clients include institutional investors and government directorates. His work is regularly featured in the *Financial Times, Evening Standard, New York Times, The Telegraph, and Washington Post*, and he is frequently a guest on such media outlets as the BBC, CNN, CNBC, and Bloomberg.

Rickards has contributed as an advisor on capital markets to the U.S. intelligence community and at the Office of the Secretary of Defense in the Pentagon. He has also testified before the U.S. House of Representatives about the 2008 financial crisis. Rickards is the author of the 2016 book The New Case for Gold and four other New York Times bestsellers.

In August 2016, Rickards explained how he reached his $10,000 target for gold in a *Daily Reckoning* report headlined "Double Digit Inflation and The Rise of Gold." The following is an excerpt.

Here Is Where The $10,000 Per Ounce Number Comes From

It's not made up. I don't throw it out there to get headlines, et cetera. It's the implied nondeflationary price of gold. Everyone says you can't have a gold standard because there's not enough gold. There's always enough gold, you just have to get the price right.

That was the mistake made by Churchill in 1925. The world is not going to repeat that mistake. I'm not saying that we will have a gold standard. I'm saying if you have anything like a gold standard, it will be critical to get the price right. To this regard, Paul Volcker said the same thing.

The analytical question is, you can have a gold standard if you get the price right; what is the non-deflationary price? What price would gold have to be to support global trade and commerce, and bank balance sheets, without reducing the money supply? The answer is $10,000 an ounce.

The math is where I use M1, based on my judgment. You can pick another measure if you choose (there are different measures of money supply). I use 40 percent backing. A lot of people don't agree with that. The Austrians say it's got to be 100 percent. Historically, it's been as low as 20 percent, so 40 percent is my number. If you take the global M1 of *the major economies, times 40 percent, and divide that by the amount of official gold in the world, the answer is approximately $10,000 an ounce.*

Now, if you go to 100 percent, you're going to get, using M1, you're going to get $25,000 an ounce. If you use M2 at 100 percent, you're going to get $50,000 an ounce. If you use 20 percent backing with M1, you're going to get $5,000 an ounce. All those numbers are going to be different based on the inputs, but just to state my inputs, I'm using global major economy M1, 40 percent backing, and official gold supply of about 35,000 tons.

Change the input, you'll change the output, but there's no mystery. It's not a made-up number. The math is eighth grade math, it's not calculus.

That's where I get the $10,000 figure. It is also worth noting that you don't have to have a gold standard, but if you do, this will be the price.

Consider that Rickards' article was written in 2016. Since then, the money supply has expanded by *at least 50%*. Maybe his gold price forecast now looks conservative to some.

And then there's the annual *In Gold We Trust* report, which I referred to in **Chapter 17 – Money Velocity and Hoarding.**

In the 2020 report, the authors present their proprietary model to forecast the gold price. Staying with the US dollar, they use M2, a broader money supply definition, which goes beyond cash and checkable bank deposits, and includes savings and time deposits, certificates of deposit, and money market funds. Then they project potential growth rates of the M2 money supply. From there they calculate the implicit gold coverage ratio by dividing the central bank's gold reserves at the current gold price by the value of M2. Ultimately, this generates the following chart.

Approximated Gold Price in 2030 by Distribution Probability, in USD

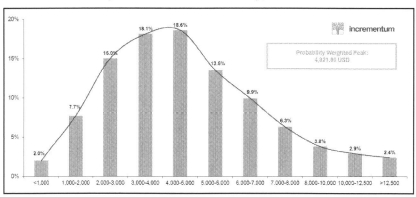

Source: Incrementum AG

The highest point in the chart is the highest probability outcome. Based on this model, Stoeferle and Valek expect the gold price to reach about $4,800 USD by 2030. However, the report goes on to state, "Not least because of the unique global debt situation described in detail in this year's *In Gold We Trust* report, growth figures for M2 in the decade that has just begun are not implausible at the same level as in the 1970s. **In this case the model suggests a gold price of $8,900 by 2030.**" (Emphasis mine)

In the 2021 *In Gold We Trust* report, the same authors suggest that if inflation should rise significantly in the next several years, a five-digit gold price ($10,000 or higher) is achievable by 2030.

There are many others, each with their own detailed case for why gold could reach $10,000 per ounce or even considerably higher.

One of my favourite tools to forecast a future gold price is simply its previous bull market.

Gold could well repeat its price action of the 1970s, which is the best and most recent secular bull market example we have. In that decade, gold went from $35 to $850, up about 24 times. Using gold's low of $260 in 2001 and applying the same multiple of 24 generates a price of $6,240.

In previous chapters, I've detailed why this bull market was likely to upstage its predecessor of 50 years ago.

Considering the current context of record sovereign debt levels, historically low interest rates and unparalleled money-printing - combined with the risks of sustained high inflation, a financial crisis, new great depression, or speculative mania - a gold rally north of $10,000 begins to sound pretty sane (and maybe even probable).

And here's what that means for silver - the metal - and all your related investments.

$300 Silver: Gold/Silver Ratio

In Chapter 32, I pointed out that the gold/silver ratio reached a mid-bull low below 30 in 1976. By the time silver peaked at $50 in January 1980, the gold/silver ratio had reached a new low of 15.

Now let's dig a little deeper to see what that might suggest going forward.

Gold/Silver Ratio 1975 - 2021

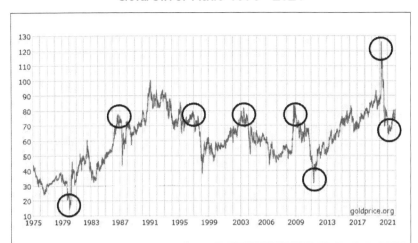

Source: goldprice.org, silverstockinvestor.com

Fast forward to the 2000s silver bull market. In April 2011, silver was once again near $50.

That's also when the gold/silver ratio touched a low near 30. I believe this ratio low, just like in the mid-1970s, marked the mid-bull peak of the secular silver bull market that began in 2001.

I think the ratio will ultimately reach a final low near 15 again in this bull market. However, I certainly don't rule out the possibility that the ratio could settle at an even-lower bottom.

My gold-peak prediction of $5,000 per ounce is just 2.5 times the August 2020 high near $2,000. Assuming $5,000 gold and an ultimate bottom in the gold/silver ratio of 15 ($5,000/15), we end up with silver trading at $333 an ounce.

Now let's assume gold goes to $10,000, like many credible prognosticators are saying. If the gold/silver ratio only reaches a final bottom near 30, as it did in 2011 ($10,000/30), we still arrive at $333 per ounce for silver.

So, using the gold/silver ratio as a guide, I believe it's

reasonable for silver to ultimately hit $300.

The following is a table that maps out several possible outcomes. It shows what silver prices would be based on various gold prices, while using several different gold/silver ratios.

Silver Prices Based on Various Gold/Silver Ratio

Gold Price	Gold/Silver Ratio							⚫ GOLDSILVER.com
	80	70	60	50	40	30	20	14 (1980 low)
$1,300	$16.25	$18.57	$21.67	$26.00	$32.50	$43.33	$65.00	$92.86
$1,500	$18.75	$21.43	$25.00	$30.00	$37.50	$50.00	$75.00	$107.14
$1,800	$22.50	$25.71	$30.00	$36.00	$45.00	$60.00	$90.00	$128.57
$2,000	$25.00	$28.57	$33.33	$40.00	$50.00	$66.67	$100.00	$142.86
$2,500	$31.25	$35.71	$41.67	$50.00	$62.50	$83.33	$125.00	$178.57
$3,000	$37.50	$42.86	$50.00	$60.00	$75.00	$100.00	$150.00	$214.29
$4,000	$50.00	$57.14	$66.67	$80.00	$100.00	$133.33	$200.00	$285.71
$5,000	$62.50	$71.43	$83.33	$100.00	$125.00	$166.67	$250.00	$357.14
$8,000	$100.00	$114.29	$133.33	$160.00	$200.00	$266.67	$400.00	$571.43
$10,000	$125.00	$142.86	$166.67	$200.00	$250.00	$333.33	$500.00	$714.29
$20,000	$250.00	$285.71	$333.33	$400.00	$500.00	$666.67	$1,000.00	$1,428.57

Source: goldsilver.com

As you can see in the rightmost column, if the ratio reaches the 1980 low, silver prices could absolutely soar to heights few can imagine today.

$300 Silver: The 1970s Prologue

As we saw earlier, the 1970s saw silver soar from a low near $1.30 in 1971 to peak at $50 in 1980. That produced an amazing 37 times *gain*, or 3,700%. Every $1,000 invested in silver at $1.30 in 1971 was worth $38,000 at the 1980 peak. That's a testament to the massive potential bull markets In silver can deliver to you.

Now let's apply the 38-fold return on the current silver bull market.

Starting with the silver low at $4.20 in 2001 - and multiply that by 38 - we get a peak of $160. Of course, this is only half of my $300 target. But I see the context and circumstances of this current bull as being an order of magnitude larger than that of

226

the 1970s. Remember, debt-to-GDP levels are a multiple of back then, debt itself has soared, and interest rates are still extremely low with many obstacles to raising them.

In my view, that's clearly enough for silver to double the performance of its previous secular bull market.

I believe we are in the second half of the bull market that began in 2001. The 1970s also experienced a mid-bull bear market. At the end of that correction, silver had bottomed at $3.97 in January 1976. It was a relatively-shallow-but-drawn-out correction.

The chart below plots several previous silver bull market cycles.

Silver Bull Markets, 100 = Start of Bull Market Cycle, 01/1971 - 05/2021

Source: Incrementum AG

The second half of the 1970s secular bull market ran from early 1976 to early 1980, when silver gained 1,130%, reaching a blow-off mania high near $50 in January 1980.

In the current secular bull market, the cycle low was in

December 2015, with silver correcting from 2011 until then. The chart above shows (gold line) by early 2021 it has only produced a smallish gain near 100%. If we use the second half of the 1970s silver bull as a proxy, then silver has much higher to go from here.

Silver bottomed in December 2015 at $15.85. Applying the same return of 1,130%, we get a very respectable $179.10.

Again, this is quite a distance from $300. But this current bull has so far taken much longer to play out than the second half of the 1970s. I think both the size and intensity of this secular bull market will far exceed that of the 1970s.

Consider debt levels back then compared with more recent ones.

U.S. Debt to GDP Ratio, 1965 - 2021

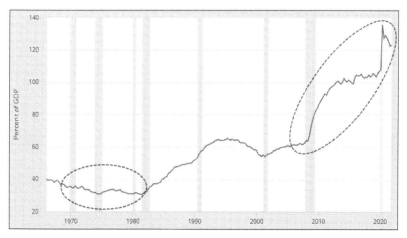

Source: Federal Reserve Bank of St. Louis, silverstockinvestor.com

We can see that U.S. debt/GDP levels in the 1970s never surpassed 35%, and fell during most of that decade, reaching a low of 30% in the early 1980s. Today, it's four times higher, at 130% of U.S. GDP, and rising.

The Institute of International Finance explains how the COVID-19 pandemic response added $24 trillion to the global debt mountain in 2020 alone, to reach a record high of $289 trillion in the first quarter of 2021. That's 360% of global GDP. And it means central banks have no choice but to try and keep rates low to avoid defaults by individual banks and entire countries.

Interest rates being maintained at 5,000-year lows will only encourage more debt. Couple that with many countries borrowing just to meet interest payments and central banks soaking up much of that new sovereign debt, and inflation havens like precious metals become very appealing.

$300 Silver: Inflation as A Driving Force

Let's look at silver price targets from another angle: inflation.

Inflation-Adjusted Silver Price 1970 - 2021

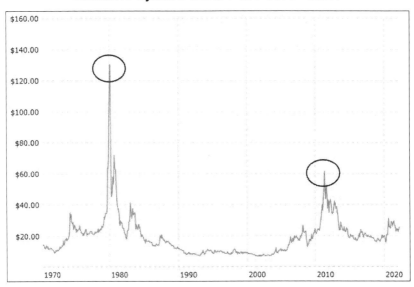

Source: macrotrends.net, silverstockinvestor.com

If we consider inflation-adjusted silver prices going back to 1970, we see that the peak reached in 1980 was $120 an ounce in today's dollars, and that's using government inflation statistics, which tend to be well below what we experience in everyday life. Even the 2011 peak of $49 is closer to $60 on an inflation-adjusted basis.

Now let's consider the old way of calculating inflation, which the United States abandoned decades ago, and I reference below (as well as in Chapter 16) from shadowstats.com. On this basis, a realistic inflation rate would have averaged 7% - 8% since 1980, which is triple the official reported average inflation rate, implying a silver price of $240-$360 dollars at the 1980 peak.

Consumer Inflation: Official vs. ShadowStats (1980-Based) Alternate

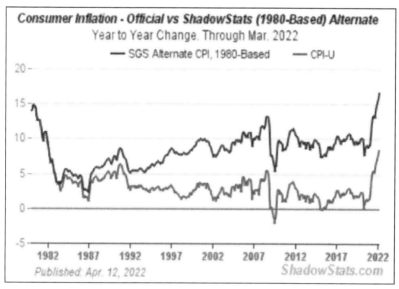

Source: shadowstats.com

My gold/silver ratio target for silver at $333 is comfortably within the range of $240-$360. If we take the midpoint between $240 and $360, we get $300. I think that's as good an estimate as any of where silver will peak in its current bull market.

$300 Silver: Silver to Gold Mining Ratio

In early 2022, silver is priced approximately 75:1 versus gold, so it takes 75 silver ounces to buy one gold ounce. But silver is being mined at much lower rates. In fact, it's lower by an order of magnitude. Consider that for each ounce of gold pulled out of the ground, just seven ounces of silver are being extracted. That's stunning, given that silver is so much cheaper than gold.

So, if we use a gold price of $1,900 and divide that by the current global mining ratio of 7, you get a price of $271.

Again, that's very close to my $300 target, and it's based on the current gold price and mining ratio. If we assume the silver to gold mining ratio remains at 7 to 1, and that the gold price continues to climb, then the $270 level becomes a minimum target price for silver.

Based on a $2,500 gold price, the 7:1 mining ratio implies a $357 silver price. And if gold ultimately reaches my target of $5,000, then the 7:1 mining ratio implies a $714 silver price. I don't know if silver will ever make it beyond $300. But these targets, based on what I consider reasonable gold prices, certainly suggest $300 silver is well within an achievable range.

$300 Silver: Home Price Predictor

In Chapter 36, I showed you the chart of silver compared to the average U.S. home price. Well, that ratio is also interesting in helping to predict a peak silver price.

Silver/Average U.S. Home Price Ratio 1975 - 2021

Source: goldsilver.com

In late-2021, the average U.S. home price was $478,000. When silver peaked in 1980 at $50, the ratio of home prices to silver bottomed at 1,464. If we use an average home price of $450,000 and divide by a ratio of 1,500 silver ounces, we get a silver price of $300. And that's without accounting for likely growth in home prices.

On this basis, the silver price would need to rise by more than 10x from current levels to reach its ultimate high.

Think about that for a moment. Consider the ripple effects of a surge that causes silver to soar 10 times from current levels. Imagine what will happen to the share prices of the companies involved in silver exploration and production - especially considering their built-in leverage.

It's not difficult to envision spectacular returns. And that's exactly why it's time to put some money to work here, albeit with a basket of stocks to make sure you catch the wave, while also spreading the risk.

Still, odds are very good that if silver goes up by a factor of 10, *the average silver stock should easily double that*, and be up by a factor of 20, while the most successful juniors could gain 50x. There are numerous cases of silver stocks that were up 100x (and more), which is a 10,000% return.

And that would simply be a repeat of previous bull markets. On its way there, you need to expect and prepare for volatility and future corrections. But you'll only benefit if you're willing to stay the course.

Key Takeaways

- I expect silver to reach $300 in this bull market, based on several indicators, including gold reaching $5,000 - $10,000.
- The gold/silver ratio, inflation adjustments, mining ratio, and silver to real estate ratio all suggest $300 silver.
- Silver stocks will likely explode higher on the way to $300 silver.

In **Part IV** we covered a lot of ground. I showed you how silver's investment characteristics make it unique.

We saw that silver had produced outstanding returns in the 1970s, as well as in the 2000s. Silver outperforms gold because it's a smaller market, it's more subject to sentiment, it's volatile, and it's the cheapest of all metals based on several indicators.

Once investors buy silver, they hang onto it. You also saw how the WallStreetBets silver squeeze event of early 2021 caused silver prices to explode and introduced silver to a whole new generation of investors.

As the precious metals bull market advances, gold gets much of the attention. New investors realize gold has risen and become expensive, so the logical alternative is more affordable silver. That helps drive a massive wave of buying in silver and silver investments.

With gold headed towards $5,000 - $10,000, inflation climbing, and its historical performance versus other assets, I expect silver to reach $300.

But all this info is only beneficial if you invest in silver.

So, in **Part V** I'll cover the entire range of silver investment options. I've invested in all of them. You'll see everything from coins and bars to junior exploration companies.

I'll show you where they stand on the risk spectrum, how silver stocks leverage the silver price, and how I build the ideal silver portfolio. I'll even give you my secrets to managing risk, and the four indicators that the silver bull market is reaching a peak.

That's important because, ultimately, you'll want to sell most of your silver investments when this bull market ends to lock in profits and reap the benefits.

The better you understand silver investing, the more profitable it will be.

Part V - Investing in Silver: The Ultimate Guide

Introduction: How to Invest in and Profit from Silver

There are many ways that you can invest in silver.

Depending on your age, risk tolerance, investment experience and comfort levels, some choices will be better suited than others.

I will cover all of these in detail.

With each silver investment option, I'll explain how it works, the benefits and disadvantages, and the relative risks. Even better, I'll show you some great techniques you can use to minimize your risk while leaving you with a lot of the gains.

I'll also describe the signposts that will eventually indicate this silver bull market is maturing and that the time to sell your silver and silver investments is approaching. Because ultimately, it's not just about generating gains but keeping those profits to help secure your financial future.

In 2020, silver prices soared in the wake of the COVID-19 pandemic. Like gold, investors flocked to silver as a safe haven against uncertainty and chaos.

Massive government stimulus programs were being announced on a scale never seen before. And this happened globally in a time frame that seemed like overnight. Central banks dramatically cut interest rates and promised to hold them at ultra-low levels if needed.

It was Modern Monetary Theory being taken to yet another level.

The U.S. Federal Reserve launched the Main Street Lending Program to support small and medium-sized businesses. The Fed also started large-scale bond purchases at a rate of $120 billion per month, also known as quantitative easing, to keep interest rates low. Other central banks launched similar programs.

Businesses were being forced to temporarily close or have employees work from home if possible. It was a gargantuan effort to stem the spread of the coronavirus. For months, all but essential services continued to operate, and even these were under strict protocols and numerous restrictions.

Not even during major wars has the global economy ever been shut down so systematically and for so long. Governments announced generous monetary support to vast swaths of the population as businesses came to a standstill and economic activity shrank dramatically. Many were forced to simply stay home, unable to go to work. And yet, the essentials like rent and food still had to be paid.

As governments developed economic stimulus programs, they quickly saw that voters were overwhelmingly on board with major infrastructure developments and a renewed fight against climate change.

So green energy programs got a massive boost. Renewable energy and electric vehicles gained widespread support. Though it's not explicitly part of their mandates, even central bankers and government treasury leaders decided to chime in.

In March of 2021, U.S. Treasury Secretary Janet Yellen called climate change "an existential threat" to the healthy functioning of the U.S. financial system. She went on, "We cannot only look back and learn the lessons of the last year. We must also look ahead at emerging risks. Climate change is obviously the big one."

During a State of the Union conference in May 2021, European Bank President Christine Lagarde said," (It) is pretty obvious, climate change will have – has already – an impact on price stability, whether you look at climate related events, whether you look at particularly exposed areas, prices will be determined as a result of that." Ensuring stable prices is part of the bank's mandate.

Naturally, this bolsters green energy initiatives and the decarbonization of energy generation and transportation. Why am I telling you all of this? Because as I explained in Chapter 25, silver is a crucial and irreplaceable metal for a vast array of green energy technologies like solar power, as well as hybrid and electric vehicles. Inevitably, the choices made on how to spend government stimulus funds will dramatically impact the demand for silver for years to come.

Seeing silver bottom at $12 in March 2020, then soar to $30 by August that year was a paradigm shift.

That's when I grasped that silver was entering the next phase of its secular bull market. And so, I decided to launch *Silver Stock Investor* (silverstockinvestor.com), dedicated exclusively to silver investing - something no other investment newsletter does. It's a holistic approach that covers everything from physical silver to junior explorers, and everything in between.

My goal was to use my decades of knowledge and experience in the silver markets to help others. I wanted to share my ongoing research on silver and silver investments.

But I also wanted to reach a wider audience to explain the magnitude of the opportunity. That's why I wrote *The Great Silver Bull.*

Right here starts the most practical part of this book.

Remember, we all have our own needs, wants, and means. There is no "right" way to go about this. I want you to understand all your investment options, their benefits, and risks, and how to go about building your ideal silver portfolio.

Like other investment sectors, silver covers the entire risk spectrum. It often makes sense to gain exposure to several of these options. Some, like physical silver, are meant to provide the most basic form of financial insurance and capital protection.

At the opposite end of the scale are junior silver explorers. These bring some of the highest risks while offering some of the highest rewards. How you combine these options within your silver investment portfolio depends on your comfort level. Just remember that, as investors, we can compensate for higher risk. One simple but very effective technique is to allocate smaller amounts to riskier investments.

You will encounter volatility. As I explained in Chapter 33, silver is a volatile asset. The prize, however, is that it can be a highly rewarding investment. Individual investors have advantages over many professional investors: time and agility. We can hold on through periods of fear when market overreaction pushes prices to unjustifiably low levels, like in March 2020. And we can react quickly and take profits when the market falls in love with a silver stock, pushing it to unrealistic and overvalued highs.

Our advantage is the strength of our conviction that silver is in a secular bull market. Armed with that mindset, we can simply wait through periods of weakness. In fact, it will sometimes make sense to be contrarian, and buy when those silver stocks become exceedingly cheap. This dramatically increases the odds in our favour: buying when assets are well below fair value and selling part or all those assets when others can't get enough of them.

I'll explain my **Silver M.A.P.** system, an easy-to-remember, simple approach to silver investing. Then, I'll show you how I think a properly diversified silver investment portfolio should be allocated. Again, this is only a guide. Your own circumstances may dictate something different for you.

The silver investment universe includes physical silver, silver ETFs, silver stock ETFs, and individual silver stocks. In addition, investors can venture into silver futures and options on silver stocks.

However, as I said earlier, these last two typically entail much higher risk. In my view, most silver investors should not invest in these areas without a lot of knowledge and experience. So instead, I'll concentrate on the first list of silver investment alternatives.

Let's start with the lowest risk: physical silver.

Chapter 41: Physical Silver

Have you ever held a pure silver coin in your hand? If not, go and buy one. You'll be impressed.

Most are beautifully crafted with intricate designs that are part shiny, part matte, and often with milled edges. A one-ounce coin has a certain weight that gives it an almost magical quality.

I especially like the ones produced by national mints for their connection to history. For instance, did you know that the United Kingdom's Royal Mint was established over 1,000 years ago, in 886, and was first located in the Tower of London?

As I explained in an earlier chapter, owning even a little physical silver is an excellent way to hold solid financial insurance that has stood the test of time. Silver is an ideal form of money because it's a precious metal like gold and shares many of its benefits. When you own silver, it's like you are your own central bank.

One of silver's most important features is that it has no counterparty risk. Unlike a stock or bond, physical silver is not someone else's liability. It's indestructible, private, can't be hacked, and retains its value. As well, the metal is fungible, meaning all silver of the same purity is essentially identical, making it a commodity. It's in limited supply, it's highly divisible, and is universally recognized and desired.

(Sidenote: silver and other precious metals are traditionally measured in troy ounces. This unit of weight is named after the city of Troyes in France. The troy ounce was commonly used in Europe during the Middle Ages, but today is only used in trading precious metals and gems. A troy ounce is about 10% heavier than the common ounce, weighing in at 1.097 oz.)

Collectible coins, also called numismatics, are a whole other market, often with sizeable premiums to the silver content because of rarity/collectability. So, buyers often pay a lot more beyond the value of the actual silver. That's not to say it isn't worthwhile, only that it takes a lot of specific knowledge and experience to do right. Investors need to be extremely well-versed in this market and to be wary of some collectible sellers. They may try to "push" a collectible coin over a bullion coin because it's good for the seller. As in any transaction, buyer beware.

Silver Bars

One option is silver bars. This is the way to get the most silver for your money. These are typically available in 10-ounce, 1 kilogram, 100-ounce, and even 1,000-ounce sizes. They are available as "generic" from lesser-known companies; however, I recommend sticking with globally recognized mints or refiners such as the Royal Canadian Mint, Engelhard, Johnson Matthey, Heraeus, and PAMP Suisse, to name a few. These will cost a little more, but you will also receive more when you sell them.

The 1,000-ounce silver bar is approximately 1,000 ounces and is typically produced by a refiner on the Good Delivery Silver Bars list, which qualifies as a COMEX acceptable/deliverable bar. COMEX is the primary futures and options market for trading silver. Traders are technically able to obtain physical delivery of silver on their futures contracts. Delivery is in the form of 1,000-ounce silver bars.

Silver Coins

My preference is for government-mint-produced bullion coins. Since they are smaller than most silver bars, it is easier to add several together to reach a desired value. They are easily recognized virtually everywhere. Size, silver content, and purity standards tend to stay constant over time, and they also benefit from the same coin remaining in production for decades.

The following are all equally good options, but it makes sense to buy coins that are either issued by your own government mint or are commonly available where you live.

Source: kitco.com

The Canadian Maple Leaf Silver one-ounce coin. It's produced by the Royal Canadian Mint and is one of the world's most recognizable silver coins. What's more, they've set the standard for purity at 0.9999 fine silver, whereas others reach only 0.999 fineness. It has a face value of $5, meaning it's worth at least CAD $5, the highest of all high-volume minted silver bullion coins. All these features combine to make it one of the world's most popular silver bullion coins. Naturally, on one side the coin has a large, detailed maple leaf, and on the reverse is the profile of Queen Elizabeth II.

Source: kitco.com

The American Eagle Silver one-ounce coin. It's been produced by the U.S. Mint since 1986 and is one of their all-time best-sellers, with over 500 million sold. It's the world's most popular 1-ounce silver bullion coin. Its weight, content and purity are all government guaranteed. After 35 years, the American Eagle was redesigned for 2021. An updated full-length figure of Liberty appears on the obverse, and a new eagle image carrying an oak branch appears on the reverse. It contains one troy ounce of 0.999 fine silver and has a face value of 1 U.S. dollar.

Source: milesfranklin.com

The Austrian Philharmonic Silver one-ounce coin. It's produced by the Austrian Mint and celebrates the Vienna Philharmonic Orchestra, depicting an assortment of musical instruments, including a string bass, cellos, violins, a harp, a Viennese horn, and a bassoon. The obverse shows the great organ of the Musikverein concert hall in Vienna. The Austrian Mint has produced tens of millions of these coins, which come at 0.999 purity and sport a face value of 1.50 euros.

When you buy any coin, consider that regular premiums on smaller silver items tend to run at about 15% above the spot price. While this isn't cheap, there are several reasons. Given that the value of an ounce of silver is relatively low, especially compared to gold, the mint's production costs are proportionally high. Government mints add a surcharge for seigniorage to cover production, distribution, and profit. Coin dealers will add their own fees associated with buying, selling, inventorying, and shipping.

Consider that premiums can vary a lot, though normally run about 12-15% above the spot price. During the 2008 financial crisis, some dealers were selling silver coins at astronomical levels of 75% above spot price. After the coronavirus pandemic struck in March 2020, mint-produced silver coins saw premiums shoot up to 50% and even higher. More than a year and a half later, these were still high in the 40%-50% range. So, economics and geopolitics can also have a big influence on premiums.

Remember to do your research before buying. Always buy from a reputable dealer and look for competitive premiums. I strongly suggest doing your own due diligence to get feedback on customer satisfaction, reliability, etc. Also, be sure to compare prices! Premiums often vary considerably from dealer to dealer. There are several long-established, well-known precious metals dealers around the world. Keep in mind that most will ship your silver, with insurance, over long distances.

If you're going to buy an "eternal asset" with major upside potential, you'll want the best. After all, you may own it for a long time. You may even pass it on to the next generation.

Junk Silver

Junk silver is a misleading term. It consists of silver U.S. quarters, dimes, and half-dollars minted pre-1965, as coins struck before that date contain 90% silver and 10% copper.

Junk Silver is sold in bags of $100 face value or $1,000 face value. Typically, the $100 face value bags contain 1,000 dimes, or 400 quarters, or 200 half-dollars (the coin denominations are usually not mixed). Since these coins were in circulation for decades, wear and tear mean they no longer contain 90% silver. Instead, they typically contain about 71.5 ounces of silver.

Why own junk silver? There are six basic reasons. 1) It's a finite commodity; it's no longer being produced (scarcity). 2) It's a product (currency coins) that is easily recognizable. 3) It's divisible, so you could use small amounts to pay for something. 4) It requires no assaying. Since it was produced by the government, everyone recognizes what you've got, so you don't need to run any tests to prove its value. 5) It's utilitarian, meaning you could use it to pay for something. 6) Many feel that, since it's declared legal tender produced by the government itself, it won't be confiscated.

A couple of other vital points. If you're Canadian, for example, keep in mind that if you buy a bag of U.S. junk silver, the market for it exists in the U.S. If you wanted to sell it in Canada, you'd probably have to accept a discount, since it's not legal tender there. However, Canadians can buy pre-1967 (junk silver) Canadian coins which were produced with about 80% silver content. These are also official Canadian legal tender and come in dimes, quarters, and half dollars.

And finally, be sure you buy from a reputable dealer. This is probably the single most crucial aspect of purchasing junk silver. Do your homework and check them out first. But don't let the name fool you; junk silver is anything but junk.

The next silver investment option is a much more recent invention: silver exchange-traded funds.

Key Takeaways

- Silver coins or bars make a great first investment.
- Do your research before buying, compare prices & service. Buyer beware!
- Junk silver - previously circulated coins - also makes for a good option.

Chapter 42: Silver ETFs

The first physically-backed gold ETF, the SPDR Gold Shares (NYSE:GLD), debuted in 2004. It was a very big deal, as it suddenly made buying and selling gold in "securitized" form easily accessible. That meant all investors, large and small, could get instant exposure to gold through their brokerage account. Each trust unit represented 1/10th the price of an ounce of gold.

Not surprisingly, its huge success spawned the birth of a similar product for gold's cousin.

The first silver exchange-traded fund soon followed in April 2006. That's when the iShares Silver Trust (NYSE:SLV) began trading. *It's since become one of the most traded commodity ETFs ever.* (Note that the acronyms ETF and ETP are typically used interchangeably).

It's important to know that not all silver ETFs are created equal. They have varying administrative and legal structures, including custodianship. Some physically backed silver ETFs offer the possibility of requesting physical delivery of the metals represented by your shares. However, in many cases, the minimum value in silver equivalent is quite large, making it impractical or inaccessible to the average investor.

In **Chapter 39 - Fallout from Silver Squeeze 2.0**, I noted some of the questions that arose in the wake of the silver squeeze events of early 2021. One of the most worrying features of some ETFs is the risk they lease out some of their silver to earn interest. That may compromise the integrity of the ETF, as two parties would have claims on the same silver at the same time. And that's troubling.

Of course, the popularity of silver ETFs is a testament to their many advantages. ETFs clearly make silver investing easy.

However, you shouldn't consider the ownership of shares in a silver ETF as equivalent to owning physical silver coins or bars. With ETFs, you have counterparty risk. You rely on the administrator to manage the trust properly, safely, and efficiently. The underlying silver is not under your personal control.

My preference amongst physically-backed silver ETFs is the **Sprott Physical Silver Trust (TSX:PSLV; NYSE:PSLV)**, which trades on the Toronto and New York Stock Exchanges. It is a closed-end trust that invests in unencumbered and fully allocated London Good Delivery ("LGD") silver bars. Sprott Asset Management is the manager, RBC Investors Services is the trustee, and the bullion custodian is the Royal Canadian Mint. Inception was in 2010, and the trust charges an annual Management Expense Ratio (MER) of 0.62% of the average daily net asset value.

As a closed-end trust, the shares can and often do trade at either a discount or a premium to the net asset value. In other words, when it trades at a discount, it's like buying silver below the spot price. When it trades at a premium, it's like buying silver above the spot price. Often, when trading at a discount, it's a sign of negative investor sentiment towards silver. The reverse is true when it trades at a premium, indicating investors are bullish on silver.

Sprott Asset Management has a longstanding, solid reputation as a precious metals and commodities-focused investment manager. Keep in mind that, although you can redeem your shares for physical silver, the minimum quantities are high. Unitholders must have enough units to equal ten 1,000 oz. silver bars. Ten thousand ounces is a lot of silver, and at $25/oz. that's the equivalent of $250,000.

The ideal time to buy is, of course, when PSLV trades at a discount. I've told my newsletter subscribers that PSLV can be an interesting alternative to physical silver when premiums are higher than normal. Investors can invest an equivalent amount in PSLV that they would have otherwise used to buy physical silver. When silver premiums are once again closer to normal levels, investors can sell their silver ETF holdings and use the proceeds to buy physical silver instead. Once again, keep in mind, a silver ETF is not the equivalent of owning physical silver.

Another silver ETF option is the Zürcher Kantonalbank's ZKB Silver ETF. It charges a management expense ratio of 0.60% and is listed on the SIX Swiss Exchange. The fund invests only in silver and is fully backed by metal. ZKB ETFs are entities that are separate from their issuers and have independent asset status as defined by the Swiss Collective Investment Schemes Act (CISA). Investors can sell their shares or redeem them for physical silver. The minimum amount for redemption purposes is high at 30 kilograms. The ZKB Silver ETF is available in three currencies: the Swiss Franc, Euro, and US dollar.

OK, so now you have a pretty good handle on how to invest in silver.

But the real action and potential are in silver stocks. As you'll see, they come in many varieties, all with their own risks and advantages.

But before I delve into that, I think it's worth understanding how we go from initially finding silver all the way to getting it out of the ground and even beyond.

Key Takeaways

- Silver ETFs are a useful, easy way to gain exposure to silver.
- Silver ETFs are not the same as physical silver, and they are not all created equal.

- The Sprott Physical Silver Trust (TSX:PSLV; NYSE:PLSV) is my favourite option.

Chapter 43: The Mining Life Cycle

It's helpful for you to understand the basics of how silver is discovered and eventually mined. Silver investments at each stage come with their own risks and rewards.

There are five basic stages of a mining project.

As **Australian Mining Consultants** explain in simplified terms, we naturally start out with exploration to find silver. If there's enough to make for a deposit that can be mined profitably, the next stage is to design and plan the mine.

The Five Basic Stages of a Mining Project

Source: amcmining.com

The mining company then needs to raise funds and build the mine. Sometimes these steps are instead for a mine expansion. That might still require exploration to find enough additional silver, then plan for and expand the existing facilities to accommodate a higher level of production.

Next is production itself. This is normally the stage when the mining company starts to generate cash flow and ultimately becomes profitable. Most mines operate for at least 6-7 years, with many having expected mine lives up to 10-15 years, and often well beyond. Some of the richest mines enjoy continuous mining for 30 years, and a rare few have produced for over a century.

These five stages of a mining project tie in directly with a concept known as the "mining life cycle." It's also referred to as the "Lassonde Curve." Pierre Lassonde is the mining legend who co-founded Franco-Nevada, the world's first gold royalty company. Some three decades ago, he created this now well-known chart.

The Life Cycle of a Mineral Discovery

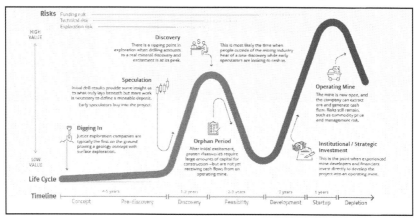

Source: Visual Capitalist

While there are countless variations, they all essentially plot the typical share price trajectory of a company that goes from concept and discovery to production and, ultimately, ore depletion.

Let's look at each in more detail.

Exploration

This is the highest risk, highest reward stage. It starts with prospecting. Explorers are out in the field, sometimes in very remote places, looking for rock outcrops or other signs of minerals. Traditional approaches like taking grab or chip samples, digging trenches, and creating visual maps are still used. But recent technology has vastly expanded the available tools.

Exploration has evolved a whole lot in recent decades.

Back in 2000, mining entrepreneur Rob McEwen was CEO of Goldcorp. Frustrated by ongoing underperformance, McEwen made a bold move. Inspired by the open-source Linux computer operating system, McEwen decided to try crowdsourcing, and make all the geological data from Goldcorp's Red Lake Gold Mine available online. The Goldcorp Challenge was born.

Many thought it was a risky, even crazy idea to reveal so much proprietary data. But McEwen ignored the critics, and it worked. A cash prize of $575,000 was enough to generate 1,000 submissions. A 3D map of the mine generated 110 deposit sites; half of which Goldcorp didn't previously know. And that led them to $6 billion of gold, making Goldcorp extremely profitable.

Today geologists can use ground or airborne surveys to better understand what may lie below the surface. Sophisticated equipment measures radiation levels, gravity, electric and magnetic fields. This allows them to detect things otherwise not apparent visually. More recently, satellite imaging tools have become indispensable, especially since the easiest discoveries have been made. There are even firms specializing in artificial intelligence to assess survey data and help make potential discoveries through more accurate drilling targets.

Next is drilling to access material below the surface in areas that have been targeted by survey, historic drilling, or mining data. That provides samples of minerals from underground, which are then sent to an assay lab to determine which elements are contained and at what concentration level.

The mining company then publishes its results. If it's a smaller company and the results are poor, the share price can fall dramatically. If results are strong or even outstanding, revealing what are called "bonanza grades," a stock can sometimes move by 50% or more in a single day.

If ongoing drilling continues to produce strong results, more speculators get drawn in, bidding up the share price. Eventually, if sufficient drilling demonstrates enough silver to make for a valuable economic deposit, the share price may reach a medium-term peak. Then, as the discovery becomes more widely known, early investors start to sell or take profits. This stage can last several years.

Development and Design

This stage requires a lot of money to put the deposit through detailed studies. Studies help determine the feasibility of building a mine to extract the minerals. That includes environmental assessments, engineering studies to figure out how the deposit would be mined, the potential layout and design of the mine, the equipment and buildings required, and staffing to run and operate the mine.

At this stage, there is often ongoing drilling to help provide a more accurate model of the deposit. Metallurgical testing determines how much of which metals can be recovered from processing. A lot of effort and resources go into relations with local communities, applying for permits to continue exploring, and even potentially purchasing additional surrounding land.

In some cases, investors and/or speculators lose interest because the excitement factor has dissipated. New drill results, even if very favourable, tend to have a diminishing overall impact on the value of the project. This can be a challenging stage even for an experienced management team.

A lot of fundraising is typically required to pay for costly studies and to keep advancing the project. Sometimes a joint venture partner, like a larger established mining company, acquires a portion of the project. They will often have the deep pockets to help pay for all the advancement work needed. In some cases, it can take up to a decade to reach this stage from initial discovery.

The exploration and development stages may occur during a

strong bull market. When that's the case, and metals prices are rising significantly, this typically adds to rising values. Investors are willing to pay more for the possibility that future mining profits will be even higher.

Construction

Deciding to build the mine is a big deal. It takes large investments, often in the hundreds of millions and even into the billions of dollars. A whole lot of effort is needed to eventually reach this point. The mining company continues to engage with stakeholders at the local, municipal, state, and federal levels. This also includes ongoing involvement with non-governmental organizations (NGOs) which may be monitoring any risks to people or the environment.

Permitting work continues as the mining company typically needs to deal with multiple governmental agencies. Things like water, power, roads, and a host of other infrastructure-related activities require permits to advance while conforming to established laws.

Mines can take different forms. Open pit is when the ore is extracted right from the surface, forming a large pit. Underground mining is when a tunnel and/or shaft starting from the surface leads miners and equipment all the way to the orebody to be removed and hauled out. Some mines begin as open pits, and as that ore becomes depleted, mining continues underground for several more years.

A fully integrated mine can include buildings to house ore crushing and separating equipment, flotation circuits, refining facilities, storage, equipment repair, and management. If the location is remote, there may even be housing facilities for miners who stay for extended periods. Timelines and budgets have to be closely tracked and respected to avoid the risks of delays and overspending.

Studies have demonstrated that investing in shares of miners *at the point of a construction decision until the first output of metal has a very high success rate.* That's because there's a sense of clarity and definitive timeline. Investors can see the company's finish line to becoming a new producer. And as the outlook for cash flow approaches, investors bid up shares as they attribute an increasingly higher value. Larger investors, like fund managers and pension funds, also come into the fray as risk continues to diminish and they seek capital gains and perhaps eventually a steady dividend.

Production

Production is when the mine finally starts to produce metal from the orebody. Pre-production activity may include a good quantity of ore that's extracted and stockpiled in preparation for the first treatment steps. Actual production startup often begins at a lower rate than the mine is ultimately designed for. A lot of fine-tuning takes place to optimize flow. It may take several months to a full year to go from first production to reach full "nameplate" capacity.

But this is the ultimate prize when a mine is running at its planned production rate. If all goes well, cash flows become material, and profits flow to the bottom line. But risks remain. Metals prices can fluctuate, and environmental concerns may surface. Ore extraction can run into an area of the deposit that is of lower or higher grade than expected, throwing off the processing and requiring adjustment.

Naturally, extracting the ore depletes reserves. Many producing mines have ongoing exploration efforts around or near the existing orebody to search for more mineable ore. Ideally, they find enough metal to replace the extracted ore and extend the mine life to several decades and even beyond.

Closure and Reclamation

If insufficient additional reserves are found, or if metals prices fall significantly for an extended period, this may lead to eventual closure. Sometimes mines are put on care and maintenance for months or years as the operator awaits higher prices to justify production.

The development of a future mine typically requires large sums of money to be set aside at the outset, to eventually reclaim the land. As responsible operators, mining companies will minimize the disturbance of land along the entire process, from exploration through to final closure. When drill rigs finish operating at a particular spot, workers will often cover the area with earth and grass seeds, making any disturbance invisible within months. Some large open pits, once depleted, become lakes that blend into their surroundings.

Although this stage does involve considerable costs, it's an integral part of responsible mining. And the resources required to complete this stage are usually set aside well in advance.

Sometimes in a renewed market cycle, an old mine can get a new life as unmined ore becomes profitable to mine once again. As well, a fresh look from a new exploration team, perhaps with newer technologies, may lead to further discoveries around the old deposit. This can result in the reopening of an old mine and potentially years or decades of new production.

21st Century Green Mining

The quality of our future on this planet depends on how we manage natural resources. And that goes way beyond caring for the environment after a mine has shut down.

Miners who don't operate responsibly should, and usually do, face serious roadblocks.

That's why I want you to understand this important aspect of silver investing. If you can assess whether a company is being a good corporate citizen, then you'll make better investment choices...and bigger profits.

So, you need to know these three letters: ESG. They stand for "environment, social, and governance." And that's how successful mining companies run their businesses today.

Mine managers and professionals are adopting these values. And that means accounting for the environment, local population, and managing responsibly throughout the planning, operating, and post-production stages.

Mines are increasingly deeper, more remote, and located in more challenging places. But thanks to advanced technologies, many are becoming greener. Managers are replacing equipment with electric, or battery powered alternatives to achieve carbon-neutral operations. They're integrating wireless communications and artificial intelligence to help build and manage lower risk and more efficient production.

Miners are getting it.

They know that socially responsible mining means proper and fair treatment of employees and locals - who are often indigenous people. Local and federal governments in most jurisdictions are becoming increasingly strict about consulting and compensating those who live and work around mines.

That's why the best mining companies involve the locals at the earliest stages and right through the mine's life. Miners set up long term agreements that prioritize locals when sourcing services and equipment, hiring, and training for skilled positions. That way they establish trust that the mine will provide responsible economic development and positive impacts in the area. And mining companies will often support the local community by contributing resources towards medical, educational, and cultural organizations.

This new approach is not just a trend, it's becoming part of company charters. That's the "governance" part. Sound management allocates significant resources to have ESG practices followed and reported to shareholders. Mining companies include regular updates on business conduct and ethics, employees' health and safety, environmental stewardship and sustainability, energy and climate impact, community relations, and local economic development.

Remember, silver is the single best conductor of heat and electricity. That makes it crucial to a host of green energy applications like solar panels, electric vehicles, and micro-electronics - all meant to lessen our carbon footprint.

Mining silver responsibly is especially relevant to achieving ESG goals. As we evolve towards a low-carbon green economy, we will need increasing amounts of silver.

Now that you understand the mining life cycle and how to mine responsibly, let's see why investing in silver stocks can be so attractive and profitable.

Key Takeaways

- Understanding the mining life cycle and ESG is valuable for investors.
- Exploration, development & design, construction, production, closure & reclamation, and mining responsibly all impact silver stock prices in different ways and to different degrees.
- Some stages offer higher potential for gain and risk.

Chapter 44: Silver Stocks = Leverage

Silver stocks come in many types and sizes.

That includes everything from large, multibillion dollar silver miners all the way down to tiny, junior nano-cap silver explorers, and everything in between.

Although they vary tremendously in size and risk, they do have one thing in common: leverage.

One main reason investors look to silver stocks is that they provide leverage to the silver price.

Now, let's get the disclaimer out of the way: leverage works both ways, on the upside and the downside. By that, I mean when silver prices rise, silver stocks tend to rise faster. But when silver prices fall, silver stocks also tend to fall faster. It's your classic double-edged sword.

What's the point? Well, when we're in a silver bull market, like now, silver rises on balance over years or decades. So, investing in silver stocks during powerful bull markets can provide huge returns. I've regularly seen junior silver explorers jump as much as 50% in a single day.

Still, it's not all rosy, all the time. Some price drops can be substantial, even during long-term silver bull markets. Junior silver stocks can experience selloffs of 20% - 50% within days or weeks. But there are ways to limit your risk, which I will explain in Chapter 52. The point is, with managed risk, silver stocks can be incredibly rewarding investments.

For now, consider this basic rule of thumb: a diversified basket of silver stocks will typically double the return of the silver price. In fact, there have been periods within bull markets when silver stocks outperformed silver by 5 to 1 or better. Some, particularly explorers who've found a potential deposit or are rapidly expanding one, can rise 50 - 100 times in a full-blown silver mania.

That's why you want to own them.

Later, we'll look at the different types of silver stocks in more detail and see what kind of potential gains each can offer. But first, I want to give you a small taste of what silver stocks can do within a silver bull market.

In my view, the short but pronounced drop in March 2020 was an outlier. The COVID-19 pandemic was a *black swan:* an unforeseeable event that gets out of control and has serious repercussions that go well beyond the normal. Black swan events are rare, have outsized impact, and are often considered obvious in hindsight.

In early 2016 silver went through a markedly strong rally phase after a drawn-out, multi-year correction. That's why I believe the end of the mid-bull silver bear market was in late 2015, along with gold.

What happened next was quite stunning. As the silver price rose, silver stocks leveraged those gains, but in dramatic fashion.

I use the Global X Silver Miners ETF (NYSE:SIL) to represent silver miners, and the iShares Silver Trust (NYSE:SLV) to represent the silver price.

Global X Silver Miners ETF (NYSE :SIL) vs. iShares Silver Trust (NYSE:SLV) January - August 2016

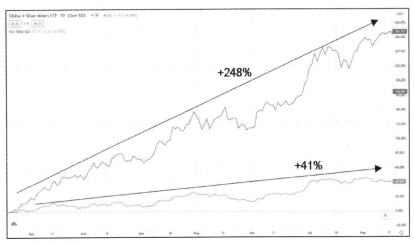

Source: Tradingview, silverstockinvestor.com

As you can see, while silver rose an impressive 41% over seven months, a basket of silver stocks rose by an astounding 248%. So, during this short period, silver stocks outperformed silver by 6 to 1. That's a great testament to the leverage of silver stocks over silver.

That's exactly why I want to own silver stocks; the leverage can be tremendous.

And to appreciate just how well silver stocks can perform during a bull market, here are a few more examples.

In November 2001, Coeur Mining (NYSE:CDE) traded down to $6.70. Within just two and a half years, Coeur had enjoyed an enormous rally all the way up to $74.10, producing a gain of 1,005%.

Coeur Mining Share Price Nov. 2001 - March 2004

+1,005%

Source: Tradingview, silverstockinvestor.com

In April of 2001, Pan American Silver (Nasdaq:PAAS; TSX:PAAS) traded down to as low as $2.52 per share. By June 2002, its share price had reached $9.22, generating a 265% gain in under a year.

Those who held on for three more years did even better. By the time we reached March of 2006, Pan American had traded all the way up to $25.60, producing a gain of 915%. That's 9 times in under five years.

In March 2008, Pan American shares had climbed higher still, trading up to $42.53 that month. Anyone holding shares from April 2001 had gained 1,587%, or nearly 16 times their original investment.

Pan American Silver Share Price April 2001 - March 2008

Source: Tradingview, silverstockinvestor.com

Then there's Wheaton Precious Metals (TSX:WPM; NYSE:WPM). Wheaton is a royalty and streaming company which does not mine for silver. Instead, they provide financing by purchasing silver royalties and streams. I'll provide more detail on this business model in a later chapter. For now, it's enough to understand that Wheaton's share price is very much leveraged to the silver price.

In November 2008, near the height of the Great Financial Crisis, Wheaton Precious Metals traded down to about $2.60. By April 2011, when silver peaked at around $49, Wheaton had soared all the way to $47. That produced a 1,700% gain in just two and a half years.

Wheaton Precious Metals Share Price
November 2008 - April 2011

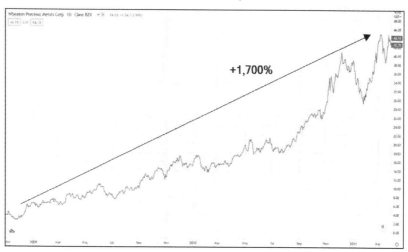

Source: Tradingview, silverstockinvestor.com

In early 2020, thanks to the COVID-19 coronavirus pandemic panic, silver and silver stocks sold off, bottoming in mid-March. But then, as people sought the safe haven of precious metals, silver and stocks soared over the next five months.

Silver gained about 150%. That was amazing.

Yet, many silver stocks did much better.

Endeavour Silver gained 316% between March and August of 2020.

Endeavour Silver Share Price March - August 2020

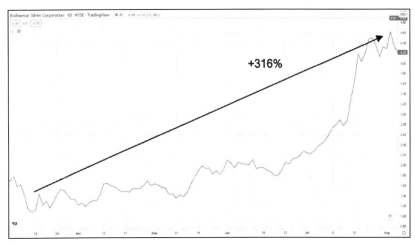

Source: Tradingview, silverstockinvestor.com

GoGold Resources (a silver producer/explorer) gained an impressive 364% in those five months.

GoGold Resources Share Price March - August 2020

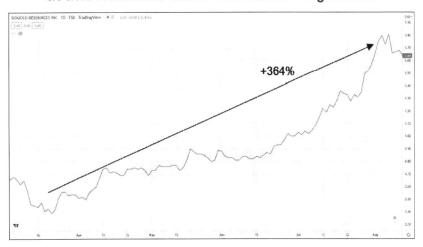

Source: Tradingview, silverstockinvestor.com

GR Silver Mining shares generated a superb 832% gain.

GR Silver Mining Share Price March - August 2020

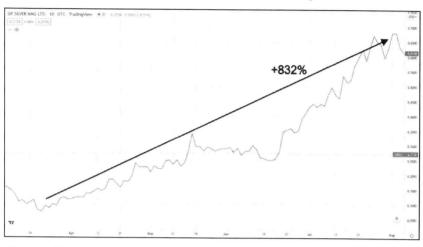

Source: Tradingview, silverstockinvestor.com

And Blackrock Silver gained an astounding 1,863% in just 5 months!

Blackrock Silver Share Price March - August 2020

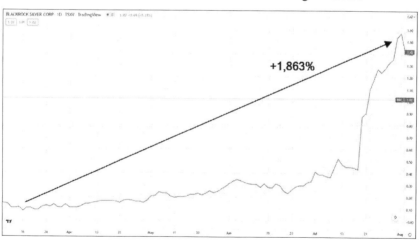

Source: Tradingview, silverstockinvestor.com

OK, by now, you get the point: silver stocks can be explosive. But it's only by being invested and buying when "the crowd" is disinterested that you'll benefit most.

Now let's look at the many ways you can invest in silver stocks.

Key Takeaways

- Silver stocks provide leverage over the silver price, both up and down.

- During silver bull markets that leverage can be as much as 6 to 1 or more.

- Even large silver companies can generate a 10x return in just a few years.

Chapter 45: Silver Miner ETFs

Some people don't have the time or the inclination to manage a portfolio of stocks, and that's okay.

If that describes you, don't worry about it. It's more important that you recognize the opportunity and act on it.

If you want instant diversification in silver stocks the simplest and fastest way is through an ETF. These hold a basket of companies engaged in acquiring, exploring, developing, and producing silver. Keep in mind that many of these miners also produce other metals like gold, copper, zinc, and lead. As I detailed in Chapter 21, only about 27% of silver comes from primary silver mines. The other 73% of silver comes as a by-product of mining other metals. Miners who get 50% or more of their revenues from silver are considered primary silver miners.

Since there aren't that many, ETF mandates allow them to invest in miners with a lower silver output while still producing substantial silver revenues. Most of the companies held in the ETFs have significant silver production, development, or exploration assets. A silver ETF investment gives the silver enthusiast instant exposure to this sector without the need to make several investment decisions.

Expenses charged by the ETF run about 0.70% annually, which is quite reasonable. The ETF usually tracks a specific mining index, and company selection depends on a minimum market capitalization, minimum daily share trading volume, and a regulated stock exchange listing. Individual stocks are limited to a maximum percentage of the overall allocation to ensure reasonable diversification. Holdings are rebalanced quarterly or semi-annually, depending on the underlying index.

I see ETFs as an excellent option, especially as you start out as a silver stock investor. You don't have to invest much, and you instantly hold several silver stocks in one investment. Naturally, silver miner ETFs provide leverage to silver. And as I showed you in the previous chapter, that leverage can be powerful, making these ETFs attractive.

Key Takeaways

- Silver Miner ETFs provide simple, instant exposure and diversification in silver stocks.

- They usually track a particular mining index and are periodically rebalanced.

- Silver Miner ETFs are a great option for investors new to the silver sector.

Chapter 46: Royalty & Streaming Companies

Royalty and streaming may just be the best, most profitable business ever invented.

Management raises money, invests up front, then sits back and cashes checks for years or even decades.

Of course, I'm exaggerating - it's never quite that simple. But this is an exceptionally attractive way to make money.

The origin of this business model in the mining sector is attributed to Franco-Nevada. In the 1980s, Pierre Lassonde (credited with the "Lassonde Curve, or Mining Life Cycle in Chapter 43) and Seymour Schulich decided to buy a 4% royalty on the revenues of a Nevada gold mine owned by Western State Minerals. Lassonde had noticed a small ad in a Reno newspaper offering the mine royalty for sale. They spent $2 million of Franco-Nevada's money to buy it, draining the company's cash. But that royalty has produced an outstanding $800 million so far. By the time it runs its course, that royalty will likely pay out a total $1.2 billion in profits.

In 2004, Wheaton River (now Wheaton Precious Metals) created the first **streaming agreement**. They made an up-front payment and contracted to receive a stream of silver delivered at a discounted price from the San Dimas gold mine in Mexico.

The royalty and streaming sector has enjoyed tremendous growth over the past couple of decades. While much smaller than traditional mining, this is an area of silver investing you need to understand, thanks to its superb business model. So, let's look at just how this subsector of mining stocks operates.

Royalty and streaming companies provide funding to mining companies whose project(s) is/are at various stages. The capital might be used to expand, advance, or even build a project. In return, the royalty/streaming company receives a portion of the miner's current or future revenue or its metal output at a big discount from the spot price.

What's the difference between royalties and streams? Royalties are often referred to as an NSR (Net Smelter Return), where the miner pays the owner of the royalty a portion of the value of the metal(s) produced or the profits generated. That typically ranges from 1-3% and lasts for the life of the mine. Even if the mine shuts down for some time or changes ownership, the royalty remains in place and effective while the mine produces.

Streams are instead a claim on the actual metal produced by the mine. The owner of the stream is entitled to receive a percentage, usually between 5% and 20%, of one or more of the metals being produced. These metals are generally purchased from the miner at a low fixed price or at a substantial percentage discount to the spot price.

Royalty and/or streaming as a source of alternative financing for mining companies can be attractive. It's neither debt nor equity, typically has a longer repayment period, and requires no fixed cash payment commitments. They don't dilute existing shareholders because the agreements don't require more shares to be issued, and usually apply to single assets. Also, streams may involve a metal or commodity that is a by-product, and therefore not central to the company's cash flows.

One big advantage royalty and streaming companies have over miners is lower risk. After all, they are not involved in exploration, permitting, building, or operating the mine. Each of those phases could bring cost overruns or climbing operating costs. Instead, their role is to evaluate a given project and then decide whether to finance it. That is the limit of their involvement. Once the asset is producing and the royalty/stream kicks in, they start to cash checks.

The business model is so efficient that the largest gold royalty companies boasted revenues per employee of over $20 million annually in 2020. By comparison Newmont and Barrick, the two largest gold producers, generated "just" $634,000 and $692,000 per employee. Odds are that this really is the most lucrative business model ever. Now, it's important to realize that investors tend to bid up their shares considerably higher than for miners because the model is so profitable. Revenues are typically strong and steady, allowing for more consistent share price gains over time.

Another advantage is geographic diversification. Many mining companies have exposure to only one or a few jurisdictions, but royalty/streaming companies can allocate globally across several projects. They can also take advantage of market downturns to acquire royalties and/or streams more cheaply, then wait for a bull market to return and generate even higher revenues in the future.

There are other upsides to this business. If a mine expands and grows its output or extends its mine life, the royalty holder will often enjoy higher and/or longer-life production. Since royalty and streaming companies can often see a return within a shorter time after investing, they can be profitable sooner. And because their cash flows are sizeable and predictable, many have a policy of paying dividends to shareholders.

As a result, they typically outperform the price of the underlying metals over time. That's because they offer leverage, and their dividends tend to be more consistent and less subject to price changes in the underlying metals.

On the other hand, mining companies tend to cut their dividends when a downturn comes to lower costs and conserve cash. During the 2013 to 2018 bear market, royalty companies outperformed mining companies as investors sought them out as stable safe havens.

Streaming Companies Outperformed Miners 2011 - 2020

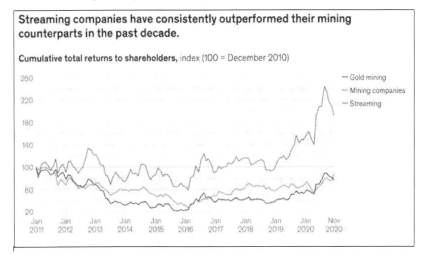

Source: McKinsey & Company

Given how their business model operates, royalty and streaming companies often have little to no debt, especially compared to their mining counterparts. McKinsey & Co. published a report in early 2021 on the streaming and royalty business. The study said the sector had expanded seven-fold over the decade preceding 2019 to reach $15 billion and was set for considerable growth over the following decade.

This is one investment option that informed silver investors must consider for solid profit potential.

Key Takeaways

- Royalty and streaming is a superb, lucrative business model.
- Royalty and streaming companies offer several advantages over miners.
- They have lower risk than miners, while offering strong leverage to the silver price.

Chapter 47: Large Producers

Large silver producers are the big guys on the block.

Now, you may be wondering; if royalty/streaming is so great, then why bother with miners?

And you'd be right, except that when we are in a strong, long term silver bull market, the miners tend to outperform their royalty/streaming peers.

They typically sport market capitalizations of $2 billion and up. They are the largest and most stable of mining companies. Usually, they have many operating mines across several jurisdictions. This helps lessen risk. When one mine runs into problems and needs to suspend operations, it often has a limited impact on the company's overall profitability. Of course, this depends on the contribution of that particular mine. By running mines in different jurisdictions, operators also minimize the impact of a particular government suspending or revoking the miner's license.

Large producers tend to have relatively predictable cash flows, and most will pay a reasonable dividend, especially during favourable market conditions. To replace depleting reserves, large miners perform ongoing exploration. Some will invest in exploration or development stage companies. They may do this through debt, cash, or by using their shares as a currency to acquire an interest in a project, partial ownership in a company, or even an outright merger or takeover.

They tend to leave the riskiest exploration, like seeking brand new discoveries, to smaller explorers. Instead, they prefer to pay a higher price to acquire part or all of a project or company once it has been sufficiently de-risked. It's typical for a large miner to simultaneously have several projects at different stages of the mine life cycle.

Big miners are sometimes amongst the largest employers, spenders, and taxpayers in some smaller nations. However, that can turn their project, which can't be moved, into a target for a hostile host country. Those governments will sometimes revoke (or threaten to revoke) operating licenses to extract more taxes or royalties from the mine owner.

Still, well-run large miners can mean big contributions to local, state and even national economies. Responsible miners are good corporate citizens that do their best to operate safely and remain respectful of the environment. Many help their local communities through various programs like building or funding hospitals, medical clinics, and schools, and by hiring and buying locally.

Key Takeaways

- Large producers are the most stable and diversified silver miners.
- They often operate multiple mines in several jurisdictions and grow internally and through mergers and acquisitions.
- Responsible miners are often big economic contributors on a local and national scale.

Chapter 48: Growing Producers & Developers

Growing producers & developers are miners that cover a wide range of size and activity. Often called "mid-tiers", they typically range from about $200 million to $2 billion in market capitalization. Since they are more growth oriented, they tend to provide more leverage to the silver price than their larger counterparts.

A growing producer will often have one or a few producing assets while advancing another project or projects. The main difference with larger producers is that the growth projects have the potential to significantly increase the miner's output.

Many will spend a large portion of their cash flow from existing operations to fund growth, whether that's on exploration to build reserves and resources, or on construction to expand or bring a new mine into production. Growing producers and developers are sometimes acquired by larger producers and can make for great medium-risk investments with strong upside potential.

Growing producers will typically provide heftier price gains during the stronger periods of a silver bull market than large producers. That's because the market begins pricing in greater future cash flows and profits at higher silver prices. Investors are willing to pay more for higher levels of future silver production. And that's what growing producers offer.

Pure developers are companies with usually a more significant, main asset that is progressing towards production. Detailed studies on the flagship asset show expected profitability of the project. The pure developer has to raise a lot of cash to get through the necessary studies, and then permit and build the mine before seeing any cash flow. They may sell off some assets considered to be of low importance to raise money and focus on their flagship project.

A high-quality management team is key. An existing producer must run the current mine(s) and oversee the new project(s) coming online. The required skill set is demanding, and deep experience with proper structure and delegation will make big a difference in achieving success.

But investing in the best-run, growing producers and developers can be very rewarding.

Key Takeaways

- Growing producers & developers have higher growth but more risk than large producers.
- They may have one flagship asset, and a few other less significant ones.
- They typically provide more leverage to silver when investors pay higher valuations for future production.

Chapter 49: Mine Studies

Let's take a break from our discussion of the types and sizes of silver companies - and take a deep dive into the business itself.

I want to give you a true insider's view.

That's because this is the best place to quickly explain the four main kinds of mine studies - the research that paves the way to working mining projects. As a silver investor, this "insider's insight" will help you better understand how far a project might be along the development timeline.

KJ Kuchling Consulting Ltd. is a top mineral industry consultancy. According to Kuchling, there are essentially four types of mining studies.

The *Conceptual Study* is an introductory, in-house study done to get a handle on the project's economics. It is not compliant with securities regulations, but it provides management with the overall potential of the project.

The *Preliminary Economic Assessment (PEA)* is the first level of study to present investors with a solid view of the scope, size, and potential economics. It is compliant with securities regulations, but it remains a rough estimate. The resource (total quantity of metal in the ground) is often still in the lower certainty *Inferred Category*, while the capital and operating costs can be as much as 40% above or below final levels. The PEA can help management compare different mining scenarios, like mining underground versus an open pit from surface, small versus larger-scale mining, etc.

The *Pre-Feasibility Study (PFS)* is only prepared using resources of a higher certainty level, being *Measured and Indicated*, rather than *Inferred*. That can mean fewer tonnes of ore than in the PEA, but with more certainty. Costing is more accurate and allows for a final decision on the development scenario to be chosen. More drilling (infill) may be required to ensure a higher level of resource accuracy. Some smaller, simpler projects with a solid PEA may not justify a PFS, jumping instead directly to a Feasibility Study.

The *Feasibility Study (FS)* is typically the final step before deciding to build and develop the project. A Feasibility Study is expensive because it is highly detailed and includes environmental and social impact studies. It covers the entire range of engineering and design, permitting, technical issues, equipment, costing, various profitability scenarios depending on costs and metals prices, and even ultimate mine closure and rehabilitation. If the goal is to sell the project, a FS might not be necessary. Many potential buyers have the means and prefer to complete this level of study in-house.

Key Takeaways

- Knowing the study stage of a project helps understand its level of progress.

- Conceptual Study is in-house and to grasp potential economics, while PEA is the first level for investors to understand the scope, size, and potential value.

- PFS is higher certainty to determine mining approach, while FS is a final step before deciding to build the project.

Chapter 50: Junior Explorers

Prospectors - people with no formal training, but a keen eye and lots of motivation - have been responsible for some of mining's biggest finds.

One recent example (and a story I just love) is a silver/base metals project discovered in Newfoundland, Canada. In 2016, a local school principal was out prospecting with his son when an outcrop of bluish rocks caught his eye.

Impressed, the educator-turned-metals-explorer wisely took samples and had them tested.

He'd hit the jackpot.

Some rocks graded nearly half a kilo of silver per metric ton. That was enough for him to stake 30 claims, later selling the project to a leading exploration company. Drilling eventually confirmed there was a lot more silver tucked beneath the principal's discovery.

The reason I so much love this story is that it's an-almost perfect tale of a Junior Explorer - veritable "moonshot stocks" where early investors can make 100x their money ... or even more.

With *my own eyes*, I have seen it happen many times.

The Junior Explorers category is the one that offers us the greatest potential returns - which is why, understandably, is also carries the highest risks.

Given that fact, let me underscore this point again: Junior Explorers are super-volatile stocks - they can experience big swings, up or down, within hours and sometimes within minutes.

All it takes is a bonanza-grade drill result on a tract with no prior exploration to ignite one of these moonshot stocks; I've seen them zoom 50%, 100% or more … in a flash.

These are typically small companies whose market caps can range from under $10 million (often called "nano caps") to $200 million. The leanest operations can include a few key people (ideally, someone with financial-markets experience and a seasoned geologist), along with a promising-but-untested property.

More-established "Juniors" can include a sizeable management team, a full-fledged board of directors, consultants, an exploration team, and several advanced projects. These can even include previously producing mines, which may simply have stopped operating due to low metals prices or depleted reserves.

In the silver sector, there are many more silver explorers than there are mid-tier and large producers. Only a small percentage of silver discoveries and projects become mines.

Sometimes that's simply because the time lag can be so long that the market cycle has already topped once the project is sufficiently advanced. By that point, if metals prices are falling, larger miners become more cautious and perhaps scale back. That will often mean limiting their own exploration spending and even shuttering certain operations. Promising projects may fizzle after encouraging launches because follow-up drilling surveys fail to confirm early results. In those cases, the deposit may not grow enough to be mined economically.

But the savvy junior miner buys these projects for pennies on the dollar, guiding them through the exploration and permitting cycle while holding spending down to spartan levels. When silver prices sufficiently rebound these once-moribund projects can zoom in value.

Greenfields vs. Brownfields Exploration

This is my last bit on the technical side. But it's helpful to understand the difference between *Greenfields* and *Brownfields Exploration*.

Greenfields Exploration is when a mineral deposit is not already known to exist. Greenfields projects can be further broken down into Grassroot or Advanced projects. Grassroot is when a geologist has an idea where a deposit might exist and directs resources to test that thesis. These resources can include satellite and fly-over surveys, and geological and geophysical prospecting and mapping on the ground. Greenfields is the highest of all exploration risk levels. According to some statistics, only one out of every 5,000 to 10,000 projects ever reach production.

Brownfields Exploration is when geologists search for deposits near or adjacent to existing or previously operating mines. This scenario has a higher potential for success. Prior exploration data often exists to help lessen risk and direct exploration towards higher probability targets. With nearby facilities to mine and process ore, any new discoveries have higher odds of being developed in the future to extend the mine life.

Junior explorers can be involved in both Greenfields and Brownfields exploration. Growing developers and large producers are more likely to be engaged in Brownfields Exploration. If they pursue Greenfields Exploration, it's often through a joint venture (JV) or simply by investing directly in a junior explorer. They tend to leave the highest risk exploration to the juniors, who can focus exclusively on this specialized type of work.

Key Takeaways

- Junior Explorers are the highest risk/reward category of silver companies.

- Greenfields Exploration is when a deposit is not already known to exist.

- Brownfields Exploration is searching for a deposit near a known deposit.

Chapter 51: Silver Stocks' Relative Performance

In Chapter 32, I introduced the Gold/Silver Ratio.

I showed you how the ratio's historical behavior can tell us whether silver looks cheap or expensive relative to gold. It can also tell us when it makes sense to increase or reduce our investment weighting towards silver versus gold.

Now I'll show you two other ratios that can help us see how silver stocks are behaving versus other related assets. Again, these comparisons can tell us a lot about sentiment and performance.

Silver Stocks/Silver Ratio

The Silver Stocks/Silver Ratio is one of my favourites. I use SIL (Global X Silver Miners ETF) as a "proxy" for silver stocks.

By plotting the returns of SIL divided by the silver price over time, we can instantly assess the relative underperformance or outperformance of silver stocks versus silver.

Silver Stocks/Silver Ratio

Source: StockCharts, silverstockinvestor.com

Here's what this chart tells us. For about two and a half years, from late 2017 until early 2019, silver stocks were underperforming the silver price as the ratio trended downwards. At that point, the trend switched in favour of silver stocks, and they began gradually outperforming silver.

Even if this change in trend were only detected several months later, when the ratio set a **higher high** in late 2019 ("Buy Signal"), it would have been a profitable time to buy silver stocks.

Have a look at the next chart of the SIL ETF to see what I mean.

SIL ETF Sept. 2016 - 2021

Source: StockCharts, silverstockinvestor.com

First, note that the 50-day moving average for SIL formed a clear low in July-August 2019 (Trend Change). This was an additional clue that silver stocks might start performing well.

Using the above Silver Stocks to Silver confirmation signal that the trend was changing to favor silver stocks over silver, you could have made an initial purchase.

And, yes, there was a big, temporary price drop shortly after. That was the market shock that came from the March 2020

COVID-19 pandemic panic.

Despite that swift pullback in the price of silver stocks, they recuperated within about six weeks and achieved new highs within months. This was the start of a new and extended leg up for silver stocks.

Silver Stocks/Gold Stocks Ratio

Now let's look at a comparison of silver stocks to gold stocks. I'll use SIL again as a proxy for silver stocks, and GDX (VanEck Vectors Gold Miners ETF) as a proxy for gold stocks.

This chart plots the price of SIL divided by the price of GDX over time.

Silver Stocks/Gold Stocks Ratio

Source: StockCharts, silverstockinvestor.com

We can see that, until late 2019, the SIL/GDX ratio was falling, with silver stocks underperforming gold stocks and establishing lower lows. In late 2019, the ratio managed a "Break Out" above the falling trendline, matching the "Buy" signal above. That suggested silver stocks were starting to outperform gold stocks and that this might be the start of a new leg up for silver stocks.

The 50-day moving average only bottomed in late June 2020 (Trend Change). This was later than the SIL/Silver ratio signal, but it did provide additional confirmation that silver stocks were beginning a new rally phase.

These are just a few of the tools I use to help guide me. Used together, they can be valuable indicators about when it may be time to initiate or add exposure in the silver investment space.

Key Takeaways

- The Silver Stocks/Silver Ratio tells us how silver stocks are performing versus silver.
- The Silver Stocks/Gold Stocks Ratio tells us how silver stocks are performing relative to gold stocks.
- Changes in trend can help you decide to increase or decrease your silver investment exposure.

Chapter 52: My Blueprint for the Ideal Silver Portfolio

One major goal with silver is to give you some diversification from your other investments.

But you also want your actual silver plays to work well, too.

In short, you want to maximize your returns while managing your risk.

No surprise there, of course. But it's the "how" you do this that's the magic elixir. And that's why I've developed an easy-to-remember way to approach silver investing.

I call it the...

Silver M.A.P. System.

The **Silver M.A.P. System** is an easy way for you to understand how to set up and manage your silver investments.

Here's how it works...

- **Silver**: for wealth protection

- **M - Miners**: for leverage

- **A - Allocate**: for diversification

- **P - Profit**: to benefit from your gains

Silver - Own some physical silver as a form of insurance and to store wealth. By now, you know just how crucial silver is in your portfolio.

Miners - Own miners for leverage over the silver price. In a secular silver bull market, it makes sense to take advantage of the extra upside from silver miners and explorers.

Allocate - Spread your holdings across several silver companies at various stages of the mining life cycle. Whether you stick with royalty companies   and large producers, or venture into developers and explorers, proper   diversification will lessen your risk.

Profit - Remember to manage your gains and take profits.

That's it. If you follow my simple, straightforward **Silver M.A.P. System**, you'll have your own "treasure map" to help you make the most of this massive silver bull market.

Now I'm going to show you how I build my ideal silver portfolio.

Remember, this is my rule of thumb - not individualized investment advice. You'll want to make some adjustments so that this meshes with your other holdings - and with your personal risk tolerance, something that varies from one person to another.

This is what I see as the best way to limit risk and maximize silver investment returns:

- 10% Physical Silver

- 50% ETF, Royalty/Streaming & Large Producers

- 20% Growing Producers & Developers

- 20% Junior Explorers

It's that simple. Now let's look at each of these allocations in more detail.

Physical Silver - 10%

I strongly believe every silver investor needs to hold some

physical sliver. You can do this with coins (my preferred option), bullion bars or even so-called "junk silver." As for coins, I'm referring to non-numismatic or non-collectible coins. These are coins such as the American Silver Eagle, with no collectible value per se. Their value is mainly in silver content. However, please note that premiums can at times be extremely high, up to triple normal levels or even more. When premiums are elevated, it may be best to buy just a small quantity and wait for premiums to return closer to normal - to about 12-15% over the spot price of silver.

If you want more exposure to silver when premiums are high, one workaround might be to buy a physically backed silver ETF. I detailed this idea in Chapter 42.

I expect that the "spot" and "futures" prices of silver will rise over time to "catch up" to the physical silver price. Remember, physical silver will always trade at a premium to spot prices because of the costs of fabrication, distribution, etc. It's just that regular premiums are closer to 12% to 15%. But when demand is strong, and supply is weak, premiums can run as high as 45% to 50%. I've seen some stretches when silver premiums reached 75% or more above the spot price for months on end.

ETFs, Royalty/Streaming & Large Producers - 50%

As I said in Chapter 45, investors who want immediate and diversified exposure to silver stocks can buy a silver miner ETF. These are attractive one-click, low-cost investment options.

Investors new to silver might want to start with silver ETFs and gradually move into buying individual stocks in silver companies as their comfort with - and knowledge of - the sector expands. There are others, but the go-to silver ETF for larger miners is the **Global X Silver Miners ETF (NYSE: SIL)**. It has about $1 billion in assets and trades about 500,000 shares per day. Then there is the **ETFMG Prime Junior Silver Miners ETF (NYSE:SILJ)**.

Although it has "Junior" in its name, most of the holdings are mid-cap and large-cap silver-mining firms. SILJ has a market cap of around $750 million and trades about 1.2 million shares daily. In short, these two ETFs are big enough and liquid-enough to be diversified investments - but still have a lot of potential upside.

Royalty/streaming companies and large producers are the largest, most-stable silver companies. Their market caps are typically $2 billion and up.

Royalty/streaming companies finance other mining operations by providing upfront cash in exchange for a royalty or "stream" on that particular asset. They don't operate mines, and so don't bear the risk of exploration, permitting, building, or operating mines. Royalty/streaming companies have several assets that contribute to their revenue while diversified by company and jurisdiction.

Large producers operate several larger mines, often across multiple jurisdictions. Both royalty/streamers and large producers continue to replace depleting reserves and grow their revenue or production; it's just that they usually do so at a slower pace than medium or smaller producers.

As a rule, I prefer not to trade these companies. Instead, once I've bought them, I intend to hold them for the length of the bull market, which can be many years. That doesn't mean I hold them forever. I may also take a partial profit if I think the shares have become vastly overvalued. If I believe the company is not well managed or I can replace it with a substantially better operator, I will also consider selling to switch into another holding.

Also important: just because these are bigger companies, don't worry that they can't deliver big returns. As we saw earlier, anyone holding Pan American Silver shares from April 2001 through March 2008 grabbed a return of 1,687%, or a 17-bagger. And Wheaton Precious Metals generated a 1,880% return in just two and a half years, between 2008 and 2011. And these are two of the biggest silver mining companies operating.

Growing Producers & Developers - 20%

Growing producers and developers can vary considerably in size, and they typically offer great leverage to the price of silver

Although they have a lower risk profile than juniors, growing producers and developers are still not as safe as large producers and royalty companies. They tend to be less profitable than their larger counterparts as they invest their cash flow back into expansion.

If they operate mines, those operations tend to be smaller. They may be engaged in brownfields exploration to grow reserves to extend a mine's productive life. If they are looking to expand existing mines, profits may be spent on costly equipment to increase processing capacity. They may also be advancing or building a flagship project or adding a mine that can take years to reach production.

But their higher growth profile typically generates a faster-rising share price when we're in a silver bull market. Faster growth can attract the attention of larger producers who themselves want to grow quickly, especially if they have a strong balance sheet and high share price. So growing producers and developers can quickly become buyout targets of larger producers, making them great medium-risk investments with a potentially hefty upside.

Junior Explorers - 20%

It's important to note here that, given how risky and volatile junior explorers tend to be, investments here should be spread across several companies.

With small market caps from less than $10 million up to about $200 million, it doesn't take a lot of buying or selling to push their share prices around. So, depending on the dollar amounts allocated, I would hold at least five names, but preferably up to 10.

Junior mining exploration companies have been called the most volatile stocks on earth. I certainly wouldn't disagree. Perhaps the only things more volatile are options and futures. That is, of course, part of their allure. By investing in them, we're shooting for very big returns.

But despite detailed, in-depth research in selecting these companies, it's impossible to know which will become the outstanding performers.

For that reason, it makes sense to hold several names. Out of 10, a few may generate 5x to 10x returns, a few others may languish, and a couple may fail. Finally, perhaps just one will produce a 20x, 50x or even 100x return. But that one "moonshot" is more than enough to give you a nice return on the overall group.

A critical aspect of the junior silver space is that, in recent years, little has been spent by silver producers to expand old mines or to start new ones.

If you want proof, just look at the sector's capital spending trends over the past few years.

Silver Miners Capex Cycle

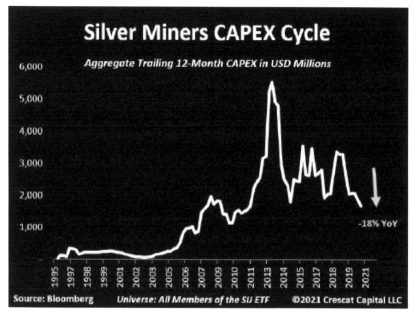

Source: Crescat Capital

Some of the spending cutbacks have been on staff, equipment, facilities, and modernization.

Still, one of the biggest cutbacks has been around exploration. Many silver miners simply chose to stop exploration spending to preserve cash during lean years, in some cases opting to mine higher-grade ore to maximize cash flow or minimize losses.

The result is many have depleted their reserves. And now that they're making loads of cash from sustained higher silver prices, they will have to spend to find more deposits through exploration or buy them outright with bolt-on acquisitions. That's what makes many junior explorers so attractive as this investment cycle ramps up. Depending on such factors as location, project quality and the regulatory environment they may become acquisition targets, leading to tremendous share price gains.

Here are a couple of other key points.

As you get better and better at this (and you will), you'll discover that a handful of names will account for a hefty (value) slice of your holdings. That's to be expected, as a few of the firms cash in on the bullish trends we've talked about here.

If you have the foresight to identify a burgeoning sector before it moves, and allocate your money across several companies, you'll have some big winners - and you'll even cash in on some mediocre ones just because silver prices have zoomed. I firmly believe that's what we've done here - targeted a promising sector before the next big leg of the bull market run has started.

And, finally, take profits. Juniors are very volatile, so they can give back a large portion or even all their gains. If a stock doubles, especially a junior miner/explorer, you can sell half. That way, you have your original stake back, and you're "playing with the house's money" - in essence, a "free ride." With a stake you've essentially acquired at zero cost, you may feel more comfortable letting that remainder ride before taking additional profits.

I believe that, by allocating across the different subsectors of the silver space, you can minimize risk and maximize returns. And by holding several companies in each subsector, you can further diversify and lower volatility.

Your goal is to preserve and grow the money you've invested. I think the approach I've outlined is the best route.

And like I showed you in **Chapter 44 - Silver Stocks = Leverage**, the gains from investing in silver stocks can be extremely rewarding. But you must be invested to benefit.

Key Takeaways

- The **Silver M.A.P. System** helps you easily set up and manage your silver investments.

- Building a portfolio with physical silver and silver stocks brings diversification and upside potential.

- It's important to identify a bull market early, then invest in it, and take profits.

Chapter 53: The Five
Secrets for Managing Risk

In the two decades I've spent watching and analyzing the markets, there's one mistake investors keep making over and over and over.

They obsess over profits - and the question: "How much can I make here?"

But they rarely ever ask the same question about risk.

I don't want you to make that same mistake.

When you invest in the right sectors (and asset classes) - and manage your risk - the "how-much-can-I-make" question takes care of itself.

There are five essential risk control tools to maximize your gains in silver and silver stocks - indeed, in any type of investment.

I'm talking about **Position-Sizing, Buying in Tranches, Playing with the House's Money, Trailing Stops,** and **Rebalancing.**

Position-Sizing

When people use the expression "don't put all your eggs in one basket," they're referring to position-sizing. It's good advice for any investment - and especially for your silver portfolio.

In **Chapter 52 - My Blueprint for the Ideal Silver Portfolio,** I showed you how I allocate capital across the different categories of silver investments: 10% physical, 50% managed investments, royalty/streaming and large producers, 20% growing producers and developers, and 20% junior explorers.

But within each of these categories, it's important to limit individual investment holdings. Starting with 100% of the capital you are planning to invest in the silver sector, the ideal breakdown I'd advocate is the following:

Silver Investments: Maximum % per Holding

Total Allocation	Category	Maximum per Holding
10%	Physical Silver	10%
50%	Managed Investments (ETFs)	10%
	Royalty/Streaming	5%
	Large Producers	5%
20%	Growing Producers & Developers	5%
20%	Junior Explorers	4%
100%	Total	

Source: silverstockinvestor.com

As you can see, I would go as high as 10% of overall portfolio allocation for managed silver investments like ETFs - because these are already diversified investments. For Royalty/Streaming and Large Producers, I would place up to 5% per company. The same goes for Growing Producers & Developers. And for Junior Explorers, I would allocate a maximum of 4% to as many as five different companies (for a maximum of 20% in "Juniors").

By carefully limiting each of these allocations, you minimize your exposure to any individual holding. If one of these investments should drop by a significant amount, its effect on the overall portfolio will be small.

Buying in Tranches

Of course, once you've decided you'll buy a particular stock, the goal is to buy it at the lowest price possible. However, only the ability to see into the future will tell you that in advance. For everyone else, there's just hindsight.

Naturally, there's just no way to know when the price has reached a near-term bottom. Still, there is a way to increase the odds that you don't overpay. It's called "layering in" or "buying in tranches."

This is a simple technique, but one very few investors follow. And yet, it's proven itself time and time again.

After years of investing and trading, I've concluded to buy at the lowest possible price when acquiring an investment. It goes like this.

> *"If you pick the bottom, you're lucky. If you layer*
> *in across the bottom, you're wise... and lucky."*

Here's a simple scenario illustrating how it can work.

Let's say you've decided the total amount you're going to commit to a new silver stock is $1,500, and each share is currently trading at $1. You could just go ahead and use the entire $1,500 to buy 1,500 shares. Or you can buy in tranches - and limit your risk of overpaying.

Let's say you divide your capital into three equal investments of $500. Next, you go ahead and buy the first tranche at $1. So, you've acquired 500 shares. Over the next few weeks, you watch those shares, and unfortunately, the price begins to fall. It's not fun seeing that investment decrease in value, but thankfully you've so far only committed the first third of your three total intended "tranches".

Two weeks go by, and the shares briefly drop down to 80 cents each - but in the next few days edge up to 85 cents each. So, you buy your second tranche of 500 shares at that 85-cent price, spending $425.

You continue to watch the 1,000 shares you now own, and the price continues to rise. Another two weeks go by, the shares are now at 95 cents, so you buy the final third of your total position. At that 95-cent price, these 500 shares cost you $475.

When you add together the cost of the three tranches, you've spent $500 + $425 + $475, for a total of $1,400. So, you've acquired the intended 1,500 shares - but at an average price of 93.33 cents each, which also saved you $100.

Of course, it doesn't always work out this way. You may buy the first tranche, and the price just keeps rising after that. So, your next two tranches may cost you more and bring up your average cost. The point is you never know.

But this technique of layering in your purchases often helps mitigate the risk of overpaying. As investors, we need to use every tool available to us, which leads me to the next tactic.

Playing With the House's Money

Here's another strategy that the wisest investors use to minimize risk.

You can use this with all the stocks in your portfolio. But I think it's imperative with junior miners and explorers. That's because these stocks are especially volatile, and their fortunes can change so quickly, sometimes depending on the next drill hole or even market sentiment.

It's straightforward - and it's based on the old investing maxim: you never lose when taking a profit. When you have substantial gains in a higher-risk stock, make a point of monetizing those gains: sell some shares.

Essentially, whenever an investment has doubled, sell half your stake. That way, you've recouped your original outlay – taking that off the table – but you're still invested at no cost and can let that investment ride.

You're "playing with the house's money" at that point, meaning you have no way to lose money.

And you don't have to wait until the shares double. A 70% gain or a 90% gain can be enough for you to take some profits. Some investors sell enough shares to lock in those gains and keep enough shares to equal the dollar amount they originally invested.

You can do whichever is most comfortable – meaning it meshes best with your personal risk tolerance.

And you can take some or all those profits and invest them in another silver stock you've been watching.

Some folks may even do this with the larger silver miners in their portfolios. I'm not against this, since we can never be sure what the future holds, especially for individual companies. Often those proceeds are used to invest in another large producer, which provides the investor with additional diversification.

Trailing Stops

The use of trailing stops can be a great way to protect your capital, while keeping a good portion of your gains.

Let's say you've bought your total position in **Miner X**. You acquired 4,000 shares using the layering in technique I just described, and your average cost per share was $1. So, your total investment is $4,000.

Over the next year, those shares rally strongly, reaching $2 each. You've held on the whole way, choosing not to sell any shares after they doubled in price. Or maybe you were just so busy you hadn't noticed. Either way, your shares are way up, your total investment is now worth $8,000, and you don't want to sell. You expect it will keep rising.

But you also don't want to give back a big chunk of those hard-won gains.

So, you decide that you're willing to sell your full position if things head south. Investors using a **trailing stop** sell their shares when they fall back by a predetermined percentage from any new high. Here's how that works.

A market correction begins, and your shares in Miner X start to slide. You've decided that any drop of 25% from the peak price reached will be the trigger for you to sell your entire position. For the sake of simplicity, I always use the closing price when calculating trailing stops, which is the last price at which the stock traded on a particular day.

From the current $2 trading price, Miner X continues to rise, and its shares reach $2.50. Then they begin to drop, falling back to $2. However, that 50-cent drop is only 20% from $2.50 closing peak, so you decide to wait.

From the $2 level, the shares begin to rise again, this time to $3 with only small pullbacks. At that point, they fall back once again and eventually reach a closing price of $2.25. That 75-cent drop is 25% from $3. So, the next day you sell your entire position.

In this example, you ended up holding the shares through the decline from $2.50 to $2, then watched them rise to $3, before dropping back to $2.25. Your 4,000 shares sold at $2.25 generated proceeds of $9,000. Had you sold at $2 per share, your proceeds would have been $8,000.

Naturally, real life doesn't always play out exactly this way.

For example, you have 4,000 shares bought at $1 each.

Unfortunately, a multiyear bear market begins, and your shares sell down steadily to 75 cents. That's a 25% drop from your purchase price, and you sell your holdings to preserve capital and cut your losses. Shares keep dropping to 50 cents and stay there for the next five years. In this case, you minimized your losses and still have $3,000 to reinvest.

The most important thing is to determine the largest decline you're willing to accept from your purchase price, or any new high, and stick to it.

Rebalancing

Rebalancing your portfolio is another technique that can help lessen your overall risk. Here's an example of how it works.

Rebalancing is essentially cashing in the gains from your winning stocks and allocating those gains to your weaker stocks - or to new opportunities that you've uncovered. However, I will only buy more of my weaker stocks if I still like them and believe they have a favourable outlook.

For simplicity, let's say you hold three silver stocks, **Miner A, Miner B** and **Miner C**. You invest $1,000 in each of these at the start of Year 1. By the end of the year, Miner A is worth $2,000, Miner B is worth $1,200, and Miner C is worth $800.

In this case, rebalancing could mean selling half of Miner A and selling $200 of Miner B. You can then use the $200 from Miner B to buy more shares of Miner C. And you can use the $1,000 of gains on Miner A to purchase shares in a fourth stock, Miner D.

At the start of Year 2, you now have four silver miners in your portfolio, with each holding worth $1,000. At the end of Year 2, you start the process over again, allocating gains to weaker stocks and/or to new investments.

Tracking Silver and Silver Investments

To follow the silver price, I go to kitco.com. This website tracks the prices of silver, gold, and other precious metals on a real-time basis.

It also provides a lot of news and commentary about precious metals, the economy, and trends you need to follow. Many contributors share some of their research for free. This is a great way to become familiar with all things silver and precious metals.

One excellent and free website to track your silver portfolio is finance.yahoo.com. It lets you create several portfolios with all the stocks you own and the dates, quantities, and purchase prices you bought and sold them at. Once created, you can track the price activity and news in the shares you hold.

It also provides you with a lot of financial information about each stock, like historical pricing, debt and cash balances, dividend information, price/earnings ratios, market capitalization, and a host of other data. You can even access detailed price charts and analyst estimates.

Key Takeaways

- Five simple techniques can help you manage risk, minimize losses, and maximize gains.
- They are Position Sizing, Buying in Tranches, Playing with the House's Money, Trailing Stops, and Rebalancing.
- Two great websites: *Kitco* to track silver prices and news, and *Yahoo! Finance* to track your portfolio and get detailed financial information.

Chapter 54: When to Sell
Your Silver and Silver Stocks

By now, it's clear you know that wise investors own some physical silver and silver stocks.

The sad fact is that we're faced with escalating uncertainty, huge-and-growing deficits, soaring debt levels, ongoing money-printing, and historically low interest rates. This is a perfect scenario for silver.

No one knows exactly how things will play out. I don't pretend to have all the answers, and you should be doubtful of anyone who gives you that impression.

What I do have is decades of experience, history on my side, and a belief system that works.

Now, as we saw with precious metals in the 1970s, all bull markets eventually peak and end. The day will come for you to sell your silver stocks and perhaps even most of your silver.

It's likely, however, that you'll always want to keep some silver - even to pass along to your kids or grandchildren. They certainly make for a nice gift.

Don't expect to sell at the exact top. That's unrealistic.

But you can get near the top. You must use the tools and clues and indicators you've gained here suggesting a possible top. A peak in sentiment will also suggest a peak in price. So, when you start hearing about silver prices on the nightly news and from talking heads on financial media, it will be time to have an eye on the exit.

You will want out when everyone else wants in. It's like the old adage: "Buy when others are fearful and sell when they are greedy."

I'm going to review a few indicators I showed you in previous chapters. You'll see how they can be used in practice.

My **Four Silver Peak Clues** are:

1. FOMO

2. Gold/Silver Ratio

3. Dow/Silver Ratio

4. Silver/Real Estate Ratio

Here's an anecdotal example telling you it may be time to sell.

Silver Peak Clue #1: FOMO

In late 1979 and early 1980, when silver prices doubled and doubled again within weeks, everyone wanted silver. To get their hands on silver, many investors were willing to stand outside banks and bullion dealers (in mid-winter), forming lines hundreds of people long for several city blocks. That was a big signal to be ready to sell.

This is when FOMO (Fear of Missing Out) kicks in, and people who don't know the first thing about silver are talking about it like they were long-time experts. They're telling everyone about how much silver has gone up in the last month or year, and how much profit they've made with their silver stocks. Most of them probably only bought within the last few weeks or months based on some social media post. It's the classic "cocktail party warning signal."

Odds are it won't be just one clue, but several screaming while a peak in silver is imminent.

We have history to show us the way. Take, for instance, the

gold/silver ratio.

Silver Peak Clue #2: Gold/Silver Ratio

Chapter 32 introduced the gold/silver ratio. It helps you determine whether silver is expensive, valued fairly, or cheap versus gold.

Gold/Silver Ratio 1975 - 2021

Source: goldprice.org, silverstockinvestor.com

But if we're studying it for clues about an ultimate peak in silver, then its action around the last secular bull market is worth reviewing.

Again, this approach offers clues - but not guarantees. In early 1980, when silver reached $50 an ounce, it rapidly outpaced gold, which itself soared towards $800. At that point, the gold/silver ratio hit a final low near 15, a level that's gone unchallenged ever since.

I think this bull market will peak with a ratio below 30 and likely near 15. If we reach my gold price target of $5,000 per ounce and silver at $300 per ounce, that implies a ratio of 16.7. That's quite close to the 1980 low of 15.

If we see anything below 30, it's time to prepare to sell.

Silver Peak Clue #3: Dow/Silver Ratio

The Dow/silver ratio is calculated by dividing the Dow Jones Industrial Average Index by the silver price.

Again, if we look at how this ratio behaved in the 1970s, we get clues about what might be in store for the current silver bull market relative to the Dow.

Dow/Silver Ratio 1970 - 2022

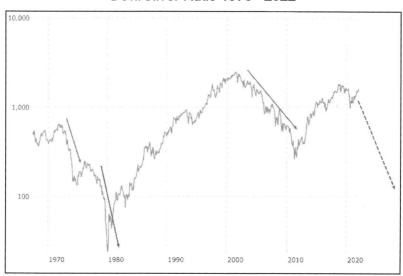

Source: macrotrends.net, silverstockinvestor.com

Here's what I want you to take away from this chart.

Between 1970 and 1980, the Dow/silver ratio experienced two long waves downward as the silver price soared and the Dow stagnated. The first low was in 1974 and the second was in 1980.

When silver finally peaked in 1980, the ratio hit a low of 24.5. That means it took just 24.5 ounces of silver (at $50/oz) to buy the Dow Jones Industrial Average Index.

The current silver bull market saw the Dow/silver ratio reach an initial low in April 2011, when silver touched $49/oz. That was the first wave down.

I believe we are entering the second wave down, which will bring a final low in the Dow/silver ratio. When silver reaches its peak price (my target being $300/oz), I expect the ratio will bottom somewhere between 25 and 100.

Once again, that will be a solid indication to consider selling your silver investments.

Silver Peak Clue #4: Silver/Real Estate Ratio

In early 2021, one of my readers sent me an account of his own experience. I think it shows just how cheap silver is, even compared to other hard assets, like real estate.

> G'day. Loved your article in Kitco. Here's a story you might want to use. We bought a lovely new detached three-bedroom house in Guernsey, U.K. in 1980 for GBP 15,000 (420 oz silver). The house is currently valued above GBP 700,000 (34,000 oz silver) that is not a typo. OK that is a generation ago, however, that statistic shows how undervalued silver currently is, OR how overvalued property has become. True value is probably somewhere in between. Might be interesting to do the same comparison for USA and Canada or even worldwide.
>
> JEFF, KITCO READER

Jeff, it seems, was spot on. The following chart is the ratio obtained by dividing the price of the average U.S. home by the price of silver. The lower the number, the less silver it takes, meaning silver is highly valued versus real estate.

Silver/Average U.S. Home Price Ratio 1975 - 2021

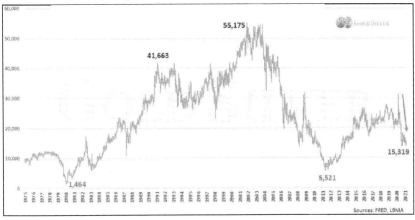

Source: goldsilver.com

A clear bottom was formed in 1980 when it took 1,464 silver ounces to buy the average U.S. home. It then peaked in the early 2000s. The silver price had languished for two decades, and it took 55,175 silver ounces to equal the cost of an average American house.

If this ratio gets to the 5,000 level or below, it will be one more indicator that it's time to have your eye on the silver exit.

Again, it's unlikely there will be a single, clear indication that silver and silver stocks have reached the top of their secular bull market. But taken together, these five indicators, along with perhaps a few others, should point to a sell signal.

I often use many of these ratios and other indicators simultaneously. This way, I can see whether silver currently appears overvalued, undervalued, or closer to fair value.

How to Sell

Remember, once you think we've reached a peak in silver prices and silver miners, it doesn't have to be an all-or-nothing proposition.

You can use the same buying in tranches tactic - but in reverse, to sell in tranches.

Let's assume you've been following the indicators described above, and you're starting to get a nagging feeling that silver is close to approaching a top.

It may be wise to sell your portfolio off in quarters or thirds. You can sell one-quarter of your holdings, then wait and watch market developments to repeat this over three months or even six months until you've liquidated everything you plan to sell.

The advantage is that you have better odds of selling across the top. And by not selling everything at once, you have the comfort of maintaining *some* exposure, while regularly reassessing the situation.

That way, if it turns out that you were early, you still get to participate in some of the ongoing upside. On the other hand, it's possible that, after having sold a portion, you decide that conditions have changed sufficiently, and you choose to hold the rest of your silver investments until a clearer sell signal has emerged.

The bottom line is that selling in tranches can improve your odds of maximizing your returns.

Key Takeaways

- Several indicators, taken together, can help assess whether silver is peaking.
- FOMO, Gold/Silver Ratio, Dow/Silver Ratio, and Silver/Real Estate Ratio can be helpful indicators of a possible silver peak.

- Selling in tranches can be a good way to minimize risk of selling too soon.

Part V was meant to show you all the nuts and bolts of investing in silver and silver stocks.

Now that you understand all these moving parts, you can make better investment decisions and build yourself a tailored silver portfolio.

We saw the different types of physical silver options, from coins to bars, and even junk silver. When it comes to silver stocks, ETFs are the simplest way to invest that also gives you instant diversification. Individual stocks or their projects can be at different stages of the mining life cycle, each of which carries its own risks and benefits.

The better you understand how mining works, the better an investor you'll be. That's why we looked at things like mine studies and the types of exploration.

But the main advantage of silver stocks is their leverage to the silver price. Using certain indicators can give you an edge.

As you build your personal silver portfolio, keep in mind my five secrets to managing risk.

The day will come when this major bull market comes to an end. My four silver peak clues will help you see if we've reached that point, and whether it's time to sell your silver investments. And finally, I showed you a few techniques you can use to lock in those profits.

I've given you all the tools you need.

Just remember, we're already in the second half of the greatest silver bull market you'll ever see.

But the biggest gains are still to come.

It's up to you.

Are you happy being an observer? Or do you want to be a participant - a "player" who profits and even cashes in big from this generational silver opportunity?

The next step is yours to take.

Conclusion

I can't emphasize enough how being invested in silver brings me comfort.

I know that silver is a solid hedge against inflation and wealth insurance. It's been a proven store of value over millennia and, unlike stocks or bonds, doesn't depend on anyone else to honor it.

It will always have intrinsic value.

Put simply, silver is the surest way I know to protect my family's financial future.

By now you've seen that silver's past gains are inspiring.

It's easy to appreciate how silver and silver stocks have made investors wildly rich during secular bull markets.

But it's the potential as we go forward in this historic bull market that has me so excited.

We're living through a period when - thanks to Modern Monetary Theory - relentless money-printing is the name of the game. Interest rates are being held near 5,000-year lows because debt levels are at historic highs and rising. Central Bank Digital Currencies are being rolled out to facilitate transactions and debt.

Governments are in a borrowing frenzy to try and keep economies afloat and stimulated. They can't afford higher interest rates because that will mean soaring payments on their ever-growing debts. At some point soon, just paying the interest will require printing more money.

There will be a crisis of confidence in fiat currencies. High-and-sustained inflation will cause people to realize their money is no longer a safe store of value. This will accelerate the death of the dollar.

In late 2021, Ray Dalio, founder of world's biggest hedge fund, told CNBC: "Cash is not a safe investment…because it will be taxed by inflation."

And that's likely to lead to another financial crisis - probably the worst one we've ever had.

The Federal Reserve is arguably the most powerful and influential financial institution on the planet. It has over 23,000 employees.

And still the last three Federal Reserve chairs - Ben Bernanke, Janet Yellen, and Jerome Powell - said they didn't see, didn't expect, or were unable to identify asset bubbles.

And yet, as I said in the introduction, several fund managers did foresee the mortgage crisis in 2008. That's why they positioned their investments to benefit from it and profited handsomely.

Just three years after former Fed Chair Janet Yellen said we would not witness another financial crisis "in our lifetimes," she was proven wrong.

In early 2020, the COVID-19 pandemic hit. It caused the global economy to be shut down for months. Within just a year and a half, the Fed's balance sheet had doubled from $4 trillion to $8 trillion. Deficits soared, and global debt hit new all-time records. Inflation, which had been falling for decades, soon reached 40-year highs.

My point is don't look to central planners to either guide you or save you. They have too many motives and restraints to give you an honest outlook, or to do what's truly best for the economy.

By manipulating interest rates and printing vast amounts of currency, central planners are often the root of the problem.

Central banks create money with no effort. A few keystrokes on their computers generate billions of dollars within seconds. They don't consult or even warn people using that currency to store their life savings.

By contrast, creating silver demands a lot of effort. And its supply is very limited. That makes silver the ultimate protection against governments as they continuously inflate the money supply to "paper over" their ongoing mistakes.

There *will* be another financial crisis. And the next one's likely to be a doozie. The excesses of the past several decades are converging towards a major financial reset on a global scale.

We are barreling towards the *largest transfer of wealth in history.*

Sadly, most people will be caught off guard - unaware and unprepared.

Don't be one of them.

Most people hold large portions of their wealth in ETFs, mutual funds, stocks, and bonds - mainly in sectors that will get hammered in the coming bear market.

Wise investors will move some of their capital into alternatives like silver, gold, and other tangibles *before* everyone else.

As most investors belatedly discover that silver and silver stocks are rising as inflation hedges, they will start investing and pushing the entire sector even higher.

That's how the largest transfer of wealth will occur. But, by investing in silver while it's *undervalued*, you're there before the herd discovers it, and lifts it to unimaginable heights.

Right now, silver and gold are dramatically under-owned.

Gold's Share of Global Assets 2020

Source: Incrementum AG

Gold represents a mere 1.1% of global assets - barely even appearing on the chart.

And silver is just 10% of the gold market.

It won't take much of a shift out of stocks and bonds, and into silver, to cause a massive surge in price.

The savviest investors - including my followers in the **Silver Stock Investor** newsletter - have already moved a portion of their capital from overvalued sectors to precious metals. Rest assured, these folks will reap the biggest windfalls.

The key is to anticipate this secular silver bull market - position some of your capital there - and then ride it as long as possible once it gets rolling.

And it *will* get rolling.

I hope you now realize that silver, prized money for thousands of years, will continue to protect investors.

It will thrive in the face of the next financial crisis, just as it has in the past.

By all accounts, we are still in the earlier stages of a secular precious-metals bull market. This book shows you why silver holds a necessary place in your portfolio. It's protection against chaos, uncertainty, and inflation.

Sure, silver will protect you during rough stretches. But silver will do **more** than serve as insurance. You can make money on it as an investment - in many forms - and that will allow you to thrive, while so many others struggle.

Silver stocks have been some of the best-performing assets ever. Under the right conditions, which we now have in spades, they become high-octane, high-return investments.

In 2020, in real time, I witnessed silver's outstanding gains in the wake of financial stresses from the coronavirus pandemic. I realized that silver's clear outperformance versus gold meant we were entering the acceleration phase of silver's bull market.

That's when everything comes together for silver as it continues to rise and even outpace gold.

I've been investing, researching, and writing about resources and precious metals for over 20 years. And I've never seen such a promising setup for silver and silver investments.

I've edited several resource newsletters and produced research covering numerous silver opportunities. I visit mines and meet with their managers and geologists to assess projects and companies for potential. My network, built up over years, has allowed me to interview scores of industry insiders.

I've contributed many articles and interviews to Forbes,

Kitco.com, BNN Bloomberg, The Financial Post, Seeking Alpha, and others. As a silver expert, I've also presented at numerous conventions and hosted and moderated panels at in-person and online mining events. And I'm a regular guest with precious metals and financial media.

All of this, along with my study of economic history, tells me silver will outperform virtually all asset classes over the next several years. People will rush to it for protection and profit as they have in the past.

When I saw the economic fallout triggered by the COVID-19 pandemic, it compelled me to share my research and insights.

So, I decided to launch a specialized silver newsletter, **Silver Stock Investor** (silverstockinvestor.com), to highlight what I'm personally buying and selling to profit from this sector.

Remember, silver is just 1/10th the size of the gold market.

It's not widely followed. And that naturally offers the potential to earn massive gains from silver and silver stocks.

We already know that gold has entered its own secular bull market, and that silver always outperforms gold.

Through **Silver Stock Investor** I share all my in-depth research and insights. That includes my views and outlook on the economy and the silver industry, as well as the companies that operate within it. More importantly, I bring actionable analysis by telling you how I'm investing my own money right now. That includes specific company recommendations, including when I see them as undervalued or overvalued.

But make no mistake, this is not mainstream research. **Silver Stock Investor** is the only investment newsletter that focuses exclusively on silver *and* covers the complete range of silver investments.

It's a detailed look at all aspects of silver and silver stock investing, aimed at filtering out biased information. I'm not paid by any of the companies in the **Silver Stock Investor** that I analyze and invest in myself.

I delve into what mines, projects, and exploration potential these companies have. I also look at the quality of their management and finances to pinpoint the very best-in-class silver producers, developers, and explorers.

Silver Stock Investor provides detailed knowledge on each stock in the portfolio, along with unbiased research and comments, as well as regular company updates.

Subscribers know what I'm doing with my own money and when I make those moves.

Remember, we're entering a market driven by massive money printing, infrastructure stimulus focused on the transition to a green economy, and the largest transfer of wealth ever.

You need silver to shelter your investment portfolio from uncertainty and inflation's detrimental effects, while benefiting from silver's explosive upside.

Closing Remarks

Writing this book has really been a labor of love.

I'm thankful to my good friend - Bill Patalon III - for planting the seed that became *The Great Silver Bull*.

I'm very fortunate and grateful for the tremendous amount of expert help I received in making this book a reality. It was challenging at times and turned out to be a much larger project than I had imagined.

That's ok because it taught me even more about silver than I already knew.

But my goal was to *share* all this knowledge with you. So, I'm glad you've made it this far.

You took a crucial step to learn about investing in silver and the essential role it plays in your financial portfolio.

It means you're an independent thinker who doesn't just take the daily drivel of most financial media. It suggests you're looking *beyond* the basic 60% stocks - 40% bonds mix as the best way to manage your retirement portfolio, especially in the years ahead.

After all - and this is vital - no one cares more about your money and financial future than you do. That's why you need to take steps to regain some control. It's also why you now recognize that silver has a place in *every* portfolio, whether your allocation is large or small.

Precious metals are one of the most solid, foundational core holdings in a truly diversified investment portfolio. Just don't expect mainstream financial advisors to know much about them, much less recommend them.

And don't be surprised if they discourage you. They often have little or nothing to gain from you buying physical silver. If you insist, they may suggest a basic silver ETF. While useful investment vehicles, silver ETFs are not a replacement for physical silver.

In the U.S. alone, online brokers hold about $20 trillion in assets. That means investors have become increasingly comfortable making their own investment decisions. Today, the internet offers unlimited amounts of information at your fingertips.

But that can become overwhelming. Knowing how to filter and interpret that information is vital.

This book is a deep dive into the *background* setting the stage for the huge silver opportunity that lies before you. I did my best to give you a solid understanding of the silver market and how silver investments work. Now you have a *framework* to build your own silver investment portfolio.

But no matter how good our forecasts might be, no one has a crystal ball to know the future with certainty. Economic and financial conditions don't always play out as we expect. As investors we need to recognize those changes and adjust for them. If you can adapt to new conditions, you'll not only survive, but prosper.

What this book *can't* do is to *follow the silver opportunity in real time*. And yet, that's a *crucial step* for you to maintain an active silver portfolio that continually fine-tunes for the inevitable changes in investment conditions.

In the *Silver Stock Investor* newsletter, I do exactly that.

I constantly research and monitor economic, market, financial and even sentiment changes to make whatever adjustments necessary. What's more, my deep experience and extensive industry network help me uncover hidden opportunities *early*, allowing for bigger returns going forward.

Because, as you realize now, the potential gains from investing in silver are outstanding. But you don't have to do this alone.

You can join the fast-growing community of *Silver Stock Investor* subscribers and follow my investment moves. It may not only help you protect your assets, but potentially generate life-changing profits from silver investments.

Take what you've learned in this book and act on it.

Buy some silver bullion coins. Invest in a silver ETF or silver stock, even with only a small amount of money.

That first step will instantly make you a silver investor and connect you to the growing community of silver enthusiasts.

Don't wait. And don't let central planners steal your financial future and comfortable retirement.

This once-in-a generation opportunity is just starting to take off.

The potential for maximum gains won't last forever.

Now's your time to profit from the greatest silver bull market ever.

About the Author

Peter Krauth is the editor of the silver-focused investment newsletter Silver Stock Investor (www.silverstockinvestor.com). Krauth has written about investing in silver for more than 20 years, using his extensive industry network to uncover outstanding opportunities.

As a precious metals expert, he is a frequent contributor to financial websites such as Kitco and Streetwise. He is a regular presenter and moderator at investment conferences, such as the Metals Investor Forum.

About Silver Stock Investor

Silver Stock Investor is written for all investors, from novice to experienced. It covers everything silver-related, from silver bullion ETFs and major silver miners, all the way to emerging high-potential junior explorers.

Each month Peter gives his thoughts on the silver market, written in a clear and concise way. He explains what's happening in silver, and provides a comprehensive look at different aspects of the silver market.

Find out more at www.silverstockinvestor.com.

Made in the USA
Columbia, SC
26 March 2023

14301921R00183